G000122643

DENMARK

BY
MARTIN SYMINGTON

Produced by AA Publishing

Written by Martin Symington

Original photography by Jesper Westley Jorgensen

Edited, designed and produced by AA Publishing.
© The Automobile Association 1996.
Maps © The Automobile Association 1996.

Distributed in the United Kingdom by AA Publishing,
Norfolk House, Priestley Road, Basingstoke, Hampshire
RG24 9NY.

A CIP catalogue record for this book is available from the
British Library.

ISBN 0 7495 1020 X

The contents of this publication are believed correct at the time of
printing. Nevertheless, the publishers cannot accept responsibility for any
errors or omissions, or for changes in the details given in this guide, or for
the consequences of any reliance on the information provided by the
same. Assessments of attractions, hotels, restaurants and so forth are
based upon the author's own experience, and therefore descriptions given
in this guide necessarily contain an element of subjective opinion which
may not reflect the publisher's opinion or dictate a reader's own
experiences on another occasion.
We have tried to ensure accuracy in this guide, but things do
change and we would be grateful if readers would advise us of any
inaccuracies they may encounter.

Published by AA Publishing (a trading name of Automobile Association
Developments Limited, whose registered office is Norfolk House,
Priestley Road, Basingstoke, Hampshire RG24 9NY. Registered number
1878835) and the Thomas Cook Group Ltd.

Colour separation: BTB Colour Reproduction, Whitchurch, Hampshire.

Printed by Edicoes ASA, Oporto, Portugal.

Cover picture: *Nyhavn, Copenhagen*
Title page: *Gilleleje harbour, Zealand*
Above: *a little girl from Fanø, an island off Jutland*

Contents

About this Book

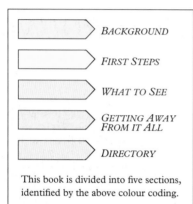

BACKGROUND

FIRST STEPS

WHAT TO SEE

GETTING AWAY FROM IT ALL

DIRECTORY

This book is divided into five sections, identified by the above colour coding.

Craftsmen on the island of Bornholm fashion original wooden toys

Background gives an introduction to the country – its history, geography, politics, culture.

First Steps offers practical advice on arriving and getting around.

What to See is an alphabetical listing of the places to visit, interspersed with walks and tours.

Getting Away From it All highlights places off the beaten track where it's possible to relax and enjoy peace and quiet.

Finally, the **Directory** provides practical information – from shopping and entertainment to children and sport. Special highly illustrated features on specific aspects of the country appear throughout the book.

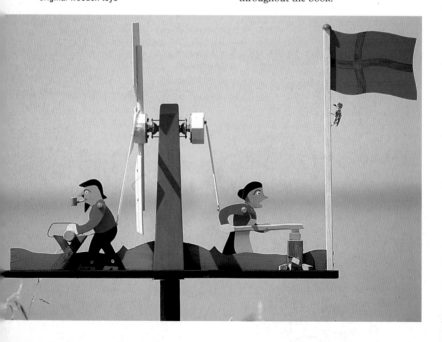

BACKGROUND

'...Denmark being the key of the Baltic...
possessing peculiar advantages for a ready
and cheap intercourse with all the
maritime nations of Europe.'

**THE ROYAL
DICTIONARY-CYCLOPAEDIA**
early 19th century

Introduction

*W*hen the world's oldest kingdom lost 40 per cent of her territory in the 1864 war with Prussia, the final nail was hammered into the coffin of an imperial nation which once ruled England and all of Scandinavia and later had colonial possessions scattered across the globe. Out of defeat, however, a new nation was born – introspective, neutral, egalitarian Denmark. Fairness, decency, tolerance and a fear of being different took root. 'What's lost abroad must be gained at home' became the country's new motto.

COUNTRY LOCATOR

Modern Denmark is a small country of a little over 5 million people, with most of her territory accounted for by the Jutland peninsula, pointing finger-like up from continental Europe, towards her Scandinavian partners, Norway and Sweden. The country's focus, however, is eastwards to Zealand, the island on which stands Copenhagen, one of Europe's great cultural cities. The Danish nation encompasses more than 400 other islands, some 90 of them inhabited.

In many ways Denmark bridges the gap between the Nordic nations and the rest of Europe. A long shared history and strong linguistic ties link Denmark with Scandinavia; in the modern era, a liberal and socially sensitive lifestyle are common to all these nations. Yet neither the Danes nor their landscape evoke the mountain and fjord ethos of, say, Norway. Instead, gentleness, undramatic beauty and freedom from extremes characterise both the land and the Danish people.

Amid this landscape are countless treasures to be discovered: ancient monuments and the remains of civilisations thousands of years old; glorious castles and fine manor houses; fishing villages of half-timbered cottages;

An Inuit Greenlander, whose homeland is part of the Danish Kingdom

DENMARK

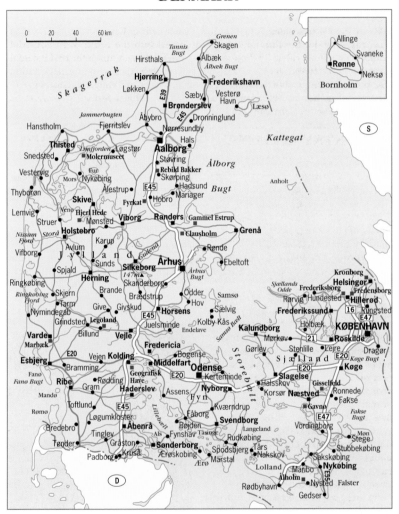

undulating hills, lakes and broad-leaved forests of the kind that inspired the fairy stories of the most famous Dane of all time – Hans Christian Andersen; endless sleepy lanes winding through the countryside, and tracing the shores of isolated fjords. All these understated gems and countless other secrets wait to be discovered by those who take Denmark to their heart.

History

Around 14,000 years ago
The earliest hunters arrive in the wake of the Ice Age.

Around 4000–1800BC
The Stone Age. Agricultural settlers grow crops and bury their dead within dolmens.

Around 1800–500BC
The Bronze Age. Skills in metalwork, ceramics and weapon-making acquired from trade with other parts of northern Europe.

Around 500BC–AD800
The Iron Age. Grauballe Man and Tollund Man interred in peat bogs near Århus and Silkeborg respectively, to be unearthed in the 1950s.

From around AD500
The Danes, a warrior tribe from Sweden, begin to settle in Jutland.

Late 8th to mid-11th centuries
The Viking era. The Danes and Norwegians raid coastal regions of England, Ireland, France, Iceland and Greenland, sometimes establishing new settlements, while others reach Russia, Turkey, North Africa and America. The spirit of the age is recorded in the sagas.

960
King Harald Bluetooth (Harald Blåtand) is baptised. Christianity takes a firm hold in Denmark.

CANUT LE GRAND

1016
The Danish King Knud (Canute) becomes King of England. Danish power is now at its apex, with much of Britain, Scandinavia and the North Sea under Viking control.

1042
Death of Hardeknud (Hardicanute), the last Danish king of England.

11th and 12th centuries
The Church grows as a political force in Denmark, in close relationship with the Crown. Huge wealth accrues through tithes; great cathedrals and thousands of stone churches are built.

1086
Knud II (Saint Canute) is murdered by rebellious peasants in Odense. His tomb later becomes a pilgrimage destination.

1157–82
King Valdemar II subjugates Norway and much of the Baltic coast.

1397
The Union of Kalmar. Denmark is united with Norway and Sweden under a single monarch, Queen Margrethe I, daughter of Valdemar II. Denmark is the dominant partner.

1523
Sweden withdraws from the Union.

1536
The Reformation. Christian III becomes king, imprisons Catholic

bishops and establishes Lutheranism throughout Denmark.

1563–70
The inconclusive Seven Years War with Sweden causes massive destruction.

1596–1648
The reign of Christian IV, Denmark's 'Golden Age'. Castles, palaces and mansions are built throughout Denmark in Renaissance style. Copenhagen becomes a major European city.

1625–57
The Thirty Years War with Sweden, launched by Christian IV to stem Swedish expansion, results in crushing defeat for Denmark and the Swedish occupation of Jutland and Funen. Hostilities cease with the signing of the Treaty of Roskilde.

1660
King Frederick III establishes absolute monarchy.

1780
Denmark joins the League of Armed Neutrality along with Russia, Prussia and Sweden.

1801–7
Nelson attacks and destroys the Danish fleet, bombards Copenhagen and occupies Zealand. Defeated Denmark sides with Napoleon.

1814
Denmark loses Norway, which is ceded to Sweden, under the Treaty of Kiel.

1848
Constitutional monarchy is established under a liberal constitution, with the new King Frederik VII handing political power to the parliament.

1864
War with Prussia leads to the loss of Schleswig-Holstein.

1914–1918
Denmark remains neutral in World War I.

1920
Parts of Schleswig (but not Holstein) are returned to Denmark under the Treaty of Versailles.

1940
The Nazi occupation of Denmark. The Danish people maintain a delicate balance of minimum co-operation in return for some measure of self government.

1943
Germany takes outright control of Denmark. The Danish Resistance Movement is born, leading to curfews, strikes and anti-Nazi violence. Thousands of Jews are heroically smuggled to Sweden.

1945
Bornholm is bombarded by Soviet forces after the Germans refuse to surrender.

1947–9
Denmark joins NATO.

1972
Frederik IX dies and is succeeded by his daughter, Margrethe II.

1973
Denmark joins the European Economic Community (today's European Union) along with the United Kingdom and the Republic of Ireland.

1979
Home rule is established in Greenland and the Faroe Islands, which remain within the Kingdom of Denmark, but outside the European Union.

1992
The Danish people reject the Maastricht Treaty on European Union in a referendum.

1993
After concessions on defence and monetary union, the Danish people vote to ratify the Maastricht Treaty in a second referendum.

THE VIKINGS

'**L**ord, deliver us from the fury of the Northmen', prayed the 9th-century Northumbrian monks after the villages and monasteries of northeastern England had been subjected to murder, rape and pillage. As brawny arms rowed fleets of longboats across the North Sea from Denmark and Norway, these attacks became increasingly frequent. Soon, no waterside town in the British Isles, France and the Iberian peninsular was safe from their ferocious attacks.

Popular myth has crowned these sea warriors with horned helmets and adorned them with fair

Myths and legends have embellished the stories of 9th-century Scandinavian adventurism

bushy beards. Over 1,000 years on, legends leave us as much in awe of their manly bravado as their butchering terrorism. But what does serious history tell us about these people and their exploits?

Killjoy though it may seem, the horns are first to go – these are pure invention. The beards, too,

were probably not universal as many Viking warriors were still boys – perhaps as young as 15. But no historian will take from them the wanton destruction and plunder of gold and silver.

However, this aspect of the Viking era is only part of the story. It is generally accepted that a population growth in Scandinavia, outstripping what the land could support, was the primary motivation for the more adventurous of these people to set sail in search of new pastures. Of much greater historical significance than their homecoming with booty was the adventuring which took Scandinavians as far afield as Constantinople (today's Istanbul, then the capital of the Byzantine Empire), North Africa, Greenland and America; and their permanent settlements – for many splendid cities, such as York and Dublin, owe their origins to the Vikings.

Vikings quickly assimilated the cultures of the countries where they settled, both contributing and absorbing skills, arts, religions and other beliefs. The English language, for example, is littered with Norse words dating from this period; even the days of the week are named after Norse gods.

Geography

*D*enmark covers an area of just over 43,000sq km, comprising the Jutland peninsula, poking finger-like northwards from Germany, the country's only land frontier, plus some 400 islands strewn across the western Baltic. About 90 of these are inhabited, including Zealand (Sjælland), the largest, with Copenhagen (København) on its eastern shore.

With more than 7,000km of coastline, and nowhere far from the sea, Denmark has been a seafaring nation since its dawn. From Viking times through to the 18th century, when Vitus Bering discovered the straits that bear his name between Russia and Alaska, Danes have been explorers. Fishing and fish processing are among the country's leading industries, supported by maritime trade with most of the world.

In the 20th century, bridge building between islands has been the impetus for engineering feats of skill and elegance; the bridge and tunnel projects spanning the Storebælt and Øresund are among the world's largest. Summer holidays, weekends and leisure time are spent sailing, or relaxing on great swathes of sandy beach.

Inland, the terrain on the Danish mainland and the islands alike is smooth, green, fecund and undramatic. The highest point (Møllehøj), in central Jutland, is just 171m above sea level; the highest waterfall a mere 18cm; there are no great rivers. But, though lacking extremes, few areas of Denmark are flat. The receding glaciers of the Ice Age left behind numerous folds of gently rolling hills.

West Jutland, facing the North Sea, has the wildest stretch of coast, marked by 300km of beach and wind-ribbed sand dunes, sprinkled with marram grass. The east coast is indented with inlets and fjords, and has a more typically Scandinavian feel. The central parts of the peninsula are characterised by moorland, lakes and undulating countryside. Only on islands such as Lolland and Falster, and on parts of the southern mainland, do you find big open skies and wind-harassed flatlands. Here, windmills for generating electricity proliferate.

Beach fringing the Kattegat sea

Funen, connected to the southeast corner of Jutland by road, is known as the 'Garden of Denmark'

Agriculture and industry

Long ago forests blanketed most of Denmark, but today only small pockets of conifer and beech wood survive, with cultivation claiming most of the countryside. About 6 per cent of Denmark's 5.1 million people are farmers or agricultural workers, and the land is largely given over to cereals, beet and other arable crops, or grazing pasture for dairy herds. Pig farming, which produces the celebrated Danish bacon, is less obviously apparent to the visitor; most of it takes place intensively and indoors.

Industry, however, has supplanted agriculture as the mainstay of Denmark's economy in recent decades. Nevertheless, compared with other developed industrial countries in Europe, its environmental impact is extraordinarily unobtrusive. Many small towns secrete their low-rise factories and light industrial units on discreet estates, shielded from view by trees and barely impinging at all on the rural landscape.

Denmark has only one major city – Copenhagen – where about 1.5 million people live. The next three largest – Århus on Jutland's east coast, Odense on Funen and Aalborg in the north of Jutland – muster not much more than half a million between them.

Lying on a latitude roughly corresponding to Scotland and southern Alaska, Denmark enjoys daylight varying from 17 hours a day in midsummer, to 7 hours in midwinter. The climate is as mild and as lacking in extremes as the landscape.

Standing defiantly outside all these generalisations are the autonomous regions of Greenland and the Faroe Islands (see pages 130–5).

Politics

Denmark is a constitutional monarchy whose sovereign, Queen Margrethe II, has reigned since 1972. Until 1953 the Danish Constitution specified that only males should ascend the throne; the constitutional change, passed by the Folketing and allowing for a sovereign queen if there were no male heirs, was ratified by referendum. The heir to the throne is Crown Prince Frederik.

Parliament

Political power is vested in the Folketing, a 179-seat parliament elected by universal adult suffrage, whose seat is in the Christiansborg Palace in Copenhagen. The voting age is 18. Members of parliament are elected on the 'first-past-the-post' system to represent the country's 135 electoral constituencies. Forty additional seats are reserved for distribution among the parties to redress the imbalance between the number of votes the parties have received nationwide, and the number of seats they have actually won (in order to be represented in the Folketing, a party must gain at least 2 per cent of the total national vote). Two further seats each are reserved for directly elected representatives from Greenland and the Faroe Islands, the two self-governing regions of Denmark.

Parliamentary terms are for a maximum of four years, although it is rare for a full term to be served. When it becomes evident that a government no longer commands a majority in the Folketing, or if a prime minister wants to put the government's case on a particular issue to the people, the procedure is to resign and call fresh elections.

At election times, posters shout their messages from Copenhagen's walls

In Roskilde, too, there is much evidence of political campaigning on the streets

Local government

Denmark has two tiers of local government. The country is divided into 14 county authorities, each with an elected county council and council chairman responsible for policies on such matters as roads and hospitals. The country is further divided into 277 municipalities, each with an elected council and mayor responsible for parochial issues.

Participation in politics

The Danes tend to be avid followers of political events, frequently paying close attention to the lengthy debates in the Folketing, that are carried live on television. Close to 90 per cent of the electorate normally exercise their vote – one of the highest figures in the world.

Recent political events

Poul Schlüter, the Conservative prime minister, took office in 1982, leading a broad coalition of parties and following policies of economic austerity in line with much of the rest of Europe. The balance of this coalition shifted a little in elections held in 1984, 1987 and 1988, though on each occasion Schlüter retained the premiership.

Denmark's rejection of the Maastricht Treaty on European political union sent shock waves around Europe and threatened the position of the pro-Maastricht prime minister. The decision was reversed, subject to some concessions, by a second referendum held the following year. By this time Schlüter had already been toppled; in January 1993 he resigned because of constitutional irregularities involved in the handling of Sri Lankan immigrants' cases by his Justice Minister.

Schlüter was replaced by Social Democratic party leader Poul Nyrup Rasmussen, heading a coalition government. Elections to the Folketing were held in September 1994 in which the Social Democrats won 63 seats, the Liberals 44, the Conservatives 28, the People's Social Party 13, the Progress Party 11, the Social Liberals 8, the Red-Green Alliance 6, the Centre Democrats 5 and independents 1. Of the 179 members returned, 120 were men and 59 women.

As leader of the party with the largest number of seats, Poul Rasmussen was asked to form a new government. He remains prime minister of a minority government in coalition with the Social Liberals and Centre Democrats. His 20-strong cabinet includes seven women.

Culture

Sooner or later most visitors to Denmark discover that the country is governed by 'Jante law'. Jante is a fictional village in which the overriding social imperative says: 'Nobody is anything special. Don't try and stand out or pretend that you are better than anybody else at anything'. Queen Margrethe once complained publicly that this attitude, typical of village life, has infected the whole country. Hence your typically cheerful, mild-mannered Dane, modestly giving controversy a wide berth.

Everybody is equal. That is what Jante law decrees. This is not an empty ideological notion, but a genuine Danish belief that leads the nation to accept a degree of social conformity that astounds other Europeans. It is, however, a conformity of Denmark's own egalitarian devising. Hence the massively high taxes, paid willingly, the almost non-existent class distinctions, and the easy interchange of traditional roles among the sexes.

A Copenhagen pedal Safari

ATTITUDES

One curious contradiction of modern Danish society is that everybody is expected to conform in tolerating different lifestyles even where these lifestyles are themselves anti-social or intolerant. The continued existence of the Christiania 'social experiment' (an all but lawless hippy commune in the centre of Copenhagen) exemplifies the paradox (see pages 30–1).

Racism and xenophobia are far smaller problems than in many parts of Europe, though nobody should be glib enough to say that they do not exist, particularly towards the growing ranks of migrant labour.

The Danish reputation for sexual promiscuity is a myth born of the Danes' genuinely liberated attitude to sexual matters (see page 35). Copenhagen's sex industry is very small scale, centring on one of Europe's least threatening red-light districts.

Copenhagen and many other Danish cities have thriving gay scenes with very low levels of animosity from the

Relaxed, informal meals at home, often taken with friends, play a large part in Danish life

heterosexual community. Gay marriage in Denmark takes the form of a legally binding agreement that gives both parties equal rights.

As far as heterosexual marriage is concerned, the institution remains popular, with around 30,000 couples tying the nuptial knot each year, usually after having first lived together. In about half these cases, couples opt for a traditional church wedding. Divorce, however, is easily obtained and about 15,000 marriages end this way each year. It is perfectly acceptable for couples to live together and bring up a family without marrying. More than 100,000 couples live in so-called 'paperless marriages' with children born of this arrangement or from previous relationships.

THE DANISH HOME

Young couples, whether married or living together, generally spend their first few years in a rented apartment. When children arrive, and if they can afford it, many then move to their own house –

usually of three or four rooms with a small garden. These are the neat modern houses, built over the last 30 years, that skirt every Danish town and city.

Inside, the décor tends to be stylish rather than traditional; among young people, modern, Danish-designed furniture is very much in vogue. The focus of every living room is the television set: it has been estimated that Danes spend 40 per cent of their leisure time in front of the small screen.

A flagpole stands in the garden of about 1 million homes, from which the red and white 'Dannebrog' flutters on national holidays, or on private occasions such as a family member's birthday.

Visitors invited inside a Danish home find that creating a feeling of *hygge* (see page 20) is central to all entertaining. Candles invariably flicker, fires burn if it is winter, and the guest is pampered. In summer, cosy gatherings on the terrace or in the garden create a similar sense of intimate sharing in family life. No greater compliment can be paid to a host than to say that you have had a *hygge* time.

Kings Garden at
Rosenborg Castle

thoughtful in their everyday dealings with each other. Even so, it is rare for men to extend extra courtesies to women just because of their sex. Standing aside to let a woman pass through a door first, for example, would be regarded as an eccentricity worthy only of a British man. On the other hand, sexual harassment tends to be less of a problem than in many parts of Europe.

RELIGIOUS OBSERVANCE

Religious observance in Denmark is low, with about 4 per cent of the population regularly attending church. Sunday services in the hundreds of beautiful churches around the country are usually attended by just a scattering of older folk, mainly women. Only at Christmas do the pews fill up.

Even so, the National Church of Denmark, which is Evangelical Lutheran, does command a genuine respect, with about 92 per cent of the population being nominal members. Despite their non-belief, it remains important for many people to be baptised, confirmed, married and buried according to church rites. More surprisingly, a special tax is levied in Denmark on behalf of the church. The equivalent of 0.8 per cent of salary, the tax is voluntary but, amazingly, 88 per cent of people pay.

SEXUAL EQUALITY

Denmark's reputation for sexual equality is, in many ways, justified. Danes are a courteous people and tend to be civil and

Child-minding and domestic chores are often shared by both partners in a household, although many women complain that their men lack enthusiasm when it comes to putting their egalitarian beliefs into practice. The law guarantees generous maternity and paternity leave, after which time both partners expect to return to work. Most couples hand the bulk of their child-minding over to public day-care centres, nurseries and kindergartens. Options such as one parent remaining at home to look after the children, or of employing a private nanny, are not only economically unfeasible to most Danes, they also break Jante law (see page 16).

In private, however, some women admit to some disquiet about the results of egalitarianism in Danish society. 'Mummy-men' is a disparaging term that has recently entered the vocabulary: it is used by women with reference to men whose masculinity has been repressed in the effort to be 'equal'.

FIRST STEPS

'Denmark's entire population
is middle-class. The truly poor
and truly rich are
so few as to be almost exotic.'
PETER HØEG
Miss Smilla's Feeling for Snow

First Steps

GETTING AROUND

Denmark is one of the easiest countries in the world for getting around. There is a fast and highly efficient air, rail, road and ferry network making virtually any part of this close-knit country accessible from anywhere else within half a day. Public transport is punctual and easy to use, generally with helpful English-speaking staff.

Information on nationwide transport is available from tourist offices. These should always be the first port of call in any city or town because of the excellent local information they provide.

Roads are well-maintained and generally adequate for the country's 1.6 million cars, with serious traffic jams a rarity. Drivers will find signposting excellent. Drivers, or indeed pedestrians, should beware, however, of straying accidently into a cycling lane. Denmark puts the cyclist on a pedestal, so to speak, and Danes regard this as an invitation to discard their native cool and courtesy, swearing like a bunch of truck drivers at transgressors!

HYGGE

Hygge is an often-used, uniquely Danish and untranslatable term. It refers to the simple cosiness and homeliness which is at the heart of Danish life. *Hygge's* obvious symbols are the candles which burn on the table at every meal, including breakfast. In practice, it means sitting round a warm fire with a blanket and a hot drink, chatting or watching television on evenings and weekends when Norwegians or Swedes would more typically be out skiing or hiking in the forest.

In the summer, cyclists are likely to find wooden trolleys left by the roadside laden with thermos flasks of iced tea, jars of honey, speckled brown eggs and other

A tourist bus on a city tour

Above and right: two-wheeled transport rules on Danish roads

homely goodies; they are left unattended, with honesty boxes to pay for whatever takes your fancy. That's *hygge*, too.

LANGUAGE

Other Scandinavians describe the Danish language as a disease of the throat. Those who try to learn it must train their vocal cords to produce rasping consonants of a kind excluded from polite conversation in most cultures, and to swallow the middle of every word. Happily for the English-speaker, nobody in Denmark expects anybody else to speak their language. English is almost universally spoken, with an extraordinary degree of fluency, making communication rarely a problem. The relationship between the English and the Danish takes the form of a sort of linguistic valve; Danes flow effortlessly into English, but the reverse is nigh on impossible.

Students at Copenhagen University take advantage of a sunny lunchtime

ETIQUETTE

Despite their great efficiency, the Danes are a casual people. Dress tends to be comfortable and functional, rather than formal or showy. Nudity is the norm on many beaches and nobody bats an eyelid; in summer when the sun shines, women feel free to sunbathe topless in city parks and other public places.

Visitors from countries where kisses and embraces are the norm sometimes find Danes socially cold. Most Danes are restrained in this regard but this should not be mistaken for lack of enthusiasm. If Danes wish to show especial warmth or affection, they are likely to do it in a small, subtle way that will be unmistakable to the recipient of the gesture, but probably unnoticed by anybody else.

LIFESTYLE

On the whole, Danes tend to be well travelled, and young people think nothing of setting off on extended back-packing journeys round the world. Five weeks' annual paid holiday is the established norm in the Danish labour market, with those who can afford it taking long-distance holidays to exotic parts of the world; hundreds of thousands more regularly head off for beach holidays in the Mediterranean or Canary Islands.

Many additional holidays are also taken within Denmark, mainly in summer cottages which people either own or rent, almost always by the sea. These are also frequently used at weekends, from spring through to the autumn.

WHAT TO SEE

'Copenhagen is as London
might be if Hyde Park
and St James's Park were
arms of the sea and
ocean-going steamers sailing
up to the gardens
of Buckingham Palace.'

BRUCE LOCKHART
My Europe

COPENHAGEN TOWN PLAN

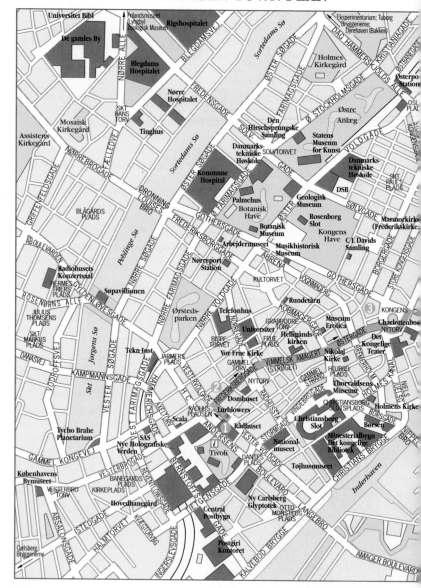

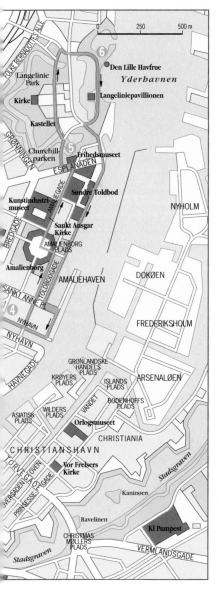

Copenhagen (København)

*C*openhagen is Scandinavia's most vibrant capital city. As the focus of Danish political, commercial and cultural life, it is, in every sense, the national capital. For many visitors – tourists and business travellers alike – Copenhagen *is* Denmark. However, as Danes unfailingly point out, this gives a false impression of the rest of the country.

Other than in the capital, Denmark is characterised by calm, understated provincialism. Some say that the vitality of the nation is sapped by Copenhagen's dominance; that the contrast between the capital and the rest of the country is absolute.

And yet many national traits, comparable with those found elsewhere in the country, are evident in Copenhagen. Small for a European capital (the population is about 1.5 million), it is uncommonly user-friendly, with many of its attractions within easy walking distance. Exploring on foot is itself a pleasure, and there are many pedestrianised streets. High-rise buildings are few and the city is characterised by green expanses and waterscapes. There is relatively little motor traffic; great store is set by pedal power as a means of urban transport, with ample tracks provided especially for cyclists.

Then and now
In the 12th century, King Valdemar I the Great gave a small fishing village, then

Denmark's imperial face shows itself at the daily changing of the Royal Guard

known simply as Havn (Harbour) to the powerful Bishop Absalon. To defend it, the bishop built a fortress on the island now known as Slotsholmen. The town grew into a key commercial port, becoming known as Købmands Havn (Merchants' Harbour), hence its present name. In 1443 it became the Danish capital, expanding hugely in the late 16th and early 17th century under the reign of Christian IV, whose grand monuments are so much part of the modern city.

Today's Copenhagen is strewn with castles, churches and other historic monuments. It also has an extraordinary wealth of museums, making it one of the richest cities anywhere for the sightseer. All this is enlivened, particularly in summer, by a thronging street scene, with outdoor cafés, restaurants and entertainers everywhere, especially along the Strøget. Stretching between Rådhuspladsen and Gammel Torv Square, this is the longest pedestrian precinct in Europe. By night, Copenhagen pulses in bars, pubs and live-music clubs.

AMALIENBORG PLADS (AMALIENBORG SQUARE)

King Frederik V has pride of place at the centre of this octagonal mosaic-cobbled piazza. He takes the form of a neoclassical equestrian statue, overlooked by the four rococo palaces that house different

Frederik V commemorated on horseback

members of the Danish royal family.

When the queen is at home, there is a daily changing of the guard ceremony. Soldiers wearing blue trousers, red tunics and huge bearskin hats keep imperial nostalgia alive, marching to the strains of a military band. The parade leaves Rosenborg castle at 11.30am daily to arrive at Amalienborg at noon.

By the Amaliehaven docks, just north of Nyhavn. None of the palaces are open to the public.

Copenhagen Tourist Information, Bernstorffsgade 1, DK - 1577 Copenhagen V (tel: 33 11 13 25).

BOTANISK HAVE (BOTANICAL GARDENS)

Wander among more than 15,500 meticulously labelled trees, shrubs and herbs in 10 hectares of landscaped gardens, originally laid out between 1871 and 1874. For tropical and sub-tropical plants there is a large domed Victorian-style greenhouse, inspired by London's Kew Gardens. Also under glass are collections of cacti, begonias, orchids and carnivorous plants.

Entrances at Gothersgade 128 and Øster Farimagsgade 2B (tel: 35 32 22 22). Entrance free. Gardens open: 25 September to 25 March, 8.30am–4pm daily; 26 March to 24 September, 8.30am–6pm daily. Admission free. Palm House open: 10am–3pm daily. Cactus House open: 1–3pm Saturday and Sunday.

Botanists from around the world seek out treasures at Botanisk Have

THE QUEEN

When a 31-year-old woman of intelligence and talent ascended the Danish throne in 1972, a palpable gust of fresh air swept through the world's oldest monarchy. Queen Margrethe II was the nation's first female monarch for nearly 600 years. With her ascension, the stuffiness characteristic of the reign of her father, Frederik IX, simply evaporated.

approved by referendum in 1953.

As queen, Margrethe involves herself directly in national affairs. Her constitutional duties as head of state involve foreign tours, regular meetings with government and diplomatic functions. She has made the most impact on Danish life, however, on issues of her own choosing. In her

In an indirect sense, Margrethe was also elected democratically; the constitutional revision allowing female succession, when there were no male heirs, was

Above and right: Queen Margrethe at her birthday celebrations
Left: the Crown Jewels of Denmark

traditional New Year address, and in frequent media interviews, she encourages her subjects to give generously to Third World charities and to take care of their own elderly. She has gently chided the nation for overdoing the 'Jante' mentality that scorns anyone who tries to stand out, suggesting that this contributes to a collective loss of self-confidence.

Most Danes listen to her with great respect. They are also proud of her many personal achievements which go beyond her monarchical duties. She has translated Simone de Beauvoir's novel *Tous les Hommes sont Mortelles* (*All Men are Mortal*) from French into Danish, and she designed the set for a television production of Hans Christian Andersen's *The Shepherdess and the Chimneysweep*. She also devotes a great deal of time to her family, including her aged mother, Queen Ingrid, her husband and consort, Prince Henrik, and her two sons, Crown Prince Frederik and Prince Joachim. Her image, however, is not one of a 'bicycling monarch'. Royal trappings, such as the changing of the guard, are maintained. She usually travels in a luxury limousine.

Few Danes will talk about their queen with anything other than affection. They might mention, in a smiling and unjudgemental way, gossip about the sexual orientation of one member of the royal family or the supposed kleptomaniac tendencies of another. Among the small minority of republican-minded Danes, many would vote for Margrethe as their first president.

CHRISTIANSBORG SLOT (CHRISTIANSBORG PALACE)

Christiansborg Palace is the cradle of Copenhagen's history and the political nerve centre of the modern state. Its origins lie in the 12th-century castle built by Bishop Absalon on the island of Slotsholmen, paving the way for Copenhagen eventually to become the capital of Denmark. Eight bridges span the canals surrounding the island.

There are still some vestiges of the original castle to explore by descending into the quiet, dank basement to see the **Palace Ruins**. The palace complex today, however, is dominated by a dense cluster of grandiose green-roofed government buildings, including the **Folketing** (the National Parliament), the prime minister's office, the Supreme Court and various royal institutions. Several of these can also be visited as individual attractions. One not to be missed is a tour (in English) of the sumptuous Renaissance Royal Reception Rooms, with their chandeliers, gilded ceilings, silk wall-hangings, priceless furniture and paintings. The rooms are still used by the queen for state occasions and official entertaining.

There is less to detain you in the Folketing, which is open to the public at certain times, even when parliament is in session. The exhibition of state coaches, in the old **Royal Stables**, is also worth a quick visit.

Christiansborg Palace Ruins (tel: 33 92 64 92). Open: October to April 9.30am–3.30pm, daily. Closed: Saturday and Monday. Admission charge.
Folketing (tel: 33 37 55 00). Open 22 June to 14 August, 10am–4pm Sunday to Friday; October to May, 10am–4pm Sunday. Admission free.

Royal Reception Rooms (tel: 33 92 64 92). English tours: June to August, 11am, 1pm and 3pm Tuesday to Sunday; May and September, 11am and 3pm Tuesday to Sunday; October to December and February to April, 11am and 3pm Tuesday and Thursday. Closed: January. Admission charge.

Royal Stables and Coaches (tel: 33 40 10 10). Open: May to September, 2–4pm Friday to Sunday: October to April, 2–4pm Saturday and Sunday. Admission charge.

Left: oarsmen row past the government buildings
Below: riotous psychedelia adorn the houses in Christiania

CHRISTIANIA

Ever since a group of hippies took over a former barracks in the Christianshavn district in 1971, declaring it to be a free state on the prevailing ideology of love, peace and flower power, Christiania has been a controversial subject in Denmark. The upshot of a clash between the parallel Danish traditions of both tolerance and social conformity was that the community should be permitted to function, subject to its own laws, as a 'social experiment'.

A quarter of a century on it is still a hang-out for social drop-outs who live there in varying degrees of permanence. There is a scruffy, laid-back ambience along the beaten earth roads and although hard drugs are outlawed, marijuana is openly sold and smoked on 'Pusher Street', the main thoroughfare.

While liberal Denmark seems basically happy with the continuing experiment, conservative opinion in the country is divided. Some people are scandalised by the fact that residents of Christiania take drugs and do not pay taxes; others believe it is useful that these elements of society are contained within a single compound.

Visitors are free to enter Christiania, wander around, buy trinkets or eat at the various cafés. Cameras, however, should be left behind; photography is not welcomed here and, on Pusher Street, it is actually banned.

Christiania is reached by Bus Number 8 from Rådhuspladsen. Alight at Prinsessegade.

HIRSCHSPRUNGSKE SAMLING (HIRSCHSPRUNGSKE COLLECTION)

Heinrich Hirschsprung (1836–1908) was a tobacco magnate, art collector and philanthropist who donated his extensive collection of mainly Danish 19th-century paintings and sculptures to the nation. The museum stands in Østre Anlæg park, to the north of the city, looking out across ornamental lakes. The collection includes many examples of the art of the Danish Golden Age, along with works by the Skagen school (see page 110) and the Funen painters (see page 73).

Stockholmsgade 29 (tel: 31 42 03 36). Open: 1–4pm Wednesday to Saturday, 11am–4pm, Sunday. Closed Monday and Tuesday. Admission charge.

LILLE HAVFRUE (LITTLE MERMAID)

Some visitors are a mite disappointed to discover that Copenhagen's most enduring symbol, a diminutive bronze figure sitting on a rock, is located in isolation in the city's industrial docks. A certain aura does surround the Little Mermaid, however, simply because she is such a celebrity, attracting a constant stream of camera-clicking admirers from around the world.

The sculpture is the work of Edvard Eriksen and depicts the title character from the Hans Christian Andersen's fairy story *The Little Mermaid*. It was donated to the city of Copenhagen in 1913 by Carl Jacobsen of the Carlsberg Breweries. The mermaid's graceful posture and modest simplicity captured the imagination of sailors. Soon, none left the port without making a pilgrimage to see her – a symbol of innocence to whom they appealed for forgiveness for their misdemeanours while in port. The sailors carried the mermaid's tale around the globe, and few tourists visit Copenhagen without seeing her.

Copenhagen was outraged in 1964 when unknown vandals decapitated the mermaid with a saw. The head was never found, so a new one was made from the original cast.

The Little Mermaid is located on a rock by the quayside about 500m north of the Amalienborg Plads.

MARMORKIRKEN (MARBLE CHURCH)

Known officially as Frederikskirken (Frederik's Church), this is Copenhagen's most arresting place of worship. Its large dome was inspired by those of St Paul's Cathedral, in London, and St Peter's Basilica, in Rome. Frederik V ordered the construction of the church in 1749. He had ambitious visions of it becoming the centrepiece of a splendid imperial district to be built around what is now Amalienborg, which he planned to call Frederiksgade.

Lack of funds put paid to the project, and work on the Marmorkirken was shelved in 1770. Finally, a rich financier, Carl Frederik Tietgen, paid for its completion in 1894. Today its imperious exterior is guarded by massive marble columns and statues of great figures from Danish history, giving the church a strong sense of being a national monument. Inside, the huge circular nave is adorned with colourful frescos.

4 Frederiksgade (tel: 33 15 37 63). Open: 11am–2pm Monday to Saturday. Admission free.

The distinctive Marmorkirken was designed as an imperial showpiece

Exhibit at the Musical History Museum, one of Copenhagen's many specialist museums

MINOR MUSEUMS

Copenhagen has scores of museums covering just about every conceivable speciality interest. Among them are museums devoted to amber, pipes and tobacco, to the history of the Danish theatre, of post and telegraphy (not to be confused with the Telephone Museum), of medical history, workers, geology, eroticism, toys, Danish Catholicism since 1654, and the history of Danish taxation. Think of a subject, however obscure, and there is a good chance that Copenhagen has, tucked away somewhere, a museum dedicated to exploring its scope, history and relevance to the modern world.

Most of these minor museums are listed in *Copenhagen This Week*, available free from the tourist office. A number deserve special mention:

Arbejdermuseet (Workers' Museum)
Shows how Danish working life and the home life of workers has changed since the 1870s.
Rømersgade 22 (tel: 33 93 25 75).

Tøjhusmuseet (Royal Arsenal Museum) This museum has a collection of weaponry and exhibitions charting the rise and fall of Denmark as an imperial power.
Tøjhusgade 3 (tel: 33 11 60 37). Closed Monday.

Musikhistorisk Museum (Musical History Museum) A superb collection of musical instruments from around the world, spanning the last 1,000 years.
Åbenrå 30 (tel: 33 11 27 26).

Zoologisk Museum (Zoological Museum) First rate, and includes a diorama of 'The Deer in the Danish Beech Forest' made with 18,000 beech leaves.
Universitetsparken 15 (tel: 35 32 10 00). Closed Monday.

Oplevelsemuseum (Believe It or Not!) Great fun for all the family, based on *Ripley's Believe It or Not* stories, with a few surprises. You have been warned!
Oplevelsemuseum Rådhuspladsen 57 (tel: 33 91 89 91).

Museum Erotica see box opposite.

Pornography

In the 1960s, while conventional mores were being re-examined all over the developed world, Denmark staked an unambiguous claim to being the most sexually liberated nation on earth. Laws banning 'pornography' were rescinded and erotic magazines, not to mention a dazzling array of sex aids and toys, became widely available.

While titillated foreign businessmen returned from Copenhagen with daring souvenirs in their briefcases, Danes took a laid-back attitude to the whole business. They were a nation that had already achieved a degree of equality between the sexes in society, way ahead of most of Europe. A liberal attitude towards sexual matters, including erotic books and films, was simply a facet of their generally enlightened social attitudes.

Since the heady days of the '60s, sexual imagery of just about every description imaginable has become commonplace all over the developed world, and in many places beyond. On the other hand attitudes among people who consider themselves 'liberal' or even 'liberated', particularly in feminist circles, have changed. Pornography stands accused of exploiting women, men, animals whatever its subjects. No longer does pornography reign as the symbol of a liberated nation.

Despite this, pornography continues to be freely available in the capital, with hard-core magazines openly for sale in ordinary newsagents, at airports or from vending machines.

Danish pornographers are no longer regarded as 'liberated'

MUSEUM EROTICA
Located in Copenhagen, this examines the history of the erotic through the ages, becoming increasingly explicit as viewers move up the building. On the top floor is the room where by far the greatest concentration of people are invariably assembled. Here, a wall is made up of television screens showing hard-core porn.

Købmagergade 24 (tel: 33 12 03 11). Open: May to September, 10am–9pm daily; October to April, 11am–6pm daily. Admission charge.

NATIONALMUSEET (NATIONAL MUSEUM)

Denmark's principal museum of culture and history reopened in 1992 in airy glass-plated glory after extensive renovation and expansion. This included covering the entrance courtyard with a glass roof to create a vast atrium surrounded by balconies.

A chronological tour of the museum starts with the rich collection of Bronze and Iron Age finds. Don't miss the golden, spiral-decorated sun worshippers' disc, mounted on a horse-drawn chariot, unearthed in Zealand and dated to about 1400BC.

Following on are rows of enigmatic rune stones, rooms full of Viking weaponry and a good section on medieval Danish life, with original peasant tools and handicrafts, plus some religious statues and gilded altarpiece carvings.

Most interesting of all, perhaps, is the **Ethnographic Collection**, with pieces from around the world, including Islamic art, oriental collections and an inspiring exhibition on Inuit life in Greenland. The latter brings the section neatly back to the museum's avowed purpose of offering 'an understanding of Denmark's relationship with the rest of the world over the last 10,000 years'.

A completely new feature is the **Children's Museum**, consisting of a variety of temporary and permanent exhibitions introducing youngsters to a glimpse of life in other cultures and other ages. A Bedouin tent and a reconstructed Viking ship, to be climbed into and played on, seem to be especial favourites.

Ny Vestergade 10 (tel: 33 13 44 11). Open: Tuesday to Sunday 10am–5pm. Admission charge.

NY CARLSBERG GLYPTOTEK (NEW CARLSBERG GALLERY)

In 1888 Carl Jacobsen of the Carlsberg brewing company donated this extensive collection of art to the nation. Jacobsen's particular fascination was with all things classical, as borne out by the rooms filled with ancient Egyptian, Greek, Roman

Copenhagen boasts a staggering array of museums, from the Carlsberg Glyptotek (left) to the New Holographic World (right)

and Etruscan relics. The art collection includes French Impressionist works by Monet, Pissaro, Degas and Cézanne and some Danish Golden Age paintings.

Dantes Plads 7 (tel: 33 41 81 41). Open: September to April, noon–3pm Tuesday to Sunday; May to August, 10am–4pm. Admission free on Wednesday and Sunday; admission charge on other days.

NYE HOLOGRAFISKE VERDEN (NEW HOLOGRAPHIC WORLD)

One of Europe's most extensive exhibitions of three-dimensional holographic pictures, this museum also charts the evolution of the art of holography. The latest exhibitions cover virtual reality, and 3D television.

Vesterbrogade 3 (tel: 33 13 17 13). Open: 27 April to 18 September, 10am–midnight daily; and 19 September to 26 April, 10am–6pm daily. Admission charge.

ORLOGSMUSEET (NAVAL MUSEUM)

This museum tells the story of the Danish Navy through 300 minutely detailed models of ships. There are also several life-sized vessels, including the Royal Barge. Some of the vessels can be boarded, and there is a play ship for children.

Overgaden oven Vandet 58A, Søkvædthuset (tel: 31 54 63 63). Open: noon–4pm Tuesday to Sunday. Admission charge.

The mysteries of the universe are revealed within the Tycho Brahe Planetarium

PLANETARIUM, TYCHO BRAHE

Europe's largest planetarium stages shows on the themes of space and cosmology. Shows begin with some gentle exploration of the universe before addressing the more challenging mysteries of the cosmos.

Gammel Kongevej 10 (tel: 33 12 12 24). Open: May to mid-June and September to April, 10.30am–9pm Tuesday to Sunday; mid-June to August 10.30am–9pm daily. Admission charge.

ROSENBORG SLOT (ROSENBORG CASTLE)

There are three compelling reasons for visiting Rosenborg. Firstly, wandering the **Rosenborg Have**, also known as the Kongens Have (King's Gardens) that surround the castle provides a superb introduction to the treasures in store. Spread over about 12 hectares, Copenhagen's oldest public park is sprinkled with statues and pavilions. From spring to summer it is ablaze with blooms that mellow into rich autumn colours.

Secondly, the small **castle** itself, built in 1606–34 by Christian IV as a summer palace outside the city walls, is a rare opportunity for an informal, almost intimate, glimpse of Danish royal life over the centuries. The tour is arranged in chronological order, through rooms stuffed with the riches accumulated by various kings. The oldest is Christian IV's Winter Room, hung with scores of Renaissance paintings; his oak-panelled and Chinese-lacquered study and his tiled bathroom have been preserved in their original state. Other highlights include Frederik IV's baroque stuccoed ceiling in the Great Hall, and his bizarre chamber with its mirrored walls and ceiling.

Finally rounding off a visit to Rosenborg, is **De Danske Kongers Kronologiste Samling** (the Danish Crown Jewels) – a separate museum in the castle basement. Pride of place among the dazzling treasures amassed by Danish royalty over the last 500 years goes to Christian IV's diamond and pearl-studded gold crown.

Øster Voldgade 4A (tel: 33 15 32 86). Castle and Crown Jewels Museum open: April, May, September and October, 11am–3pm daily; June to August, 10am–4pm daily. From November to April, the castle is only open 11am–2pm Tuesday, Friday and Sunday, and the Crown Jewels 11am–3pm Tuesday to Sunday. Admission charge.

RUNDETÅRN (ROUND TOWER)

This sturdy circular tower is one of Copenhagen's most distinctive landmarks, commanding views over the whole city and beyond from the platform at its 35m summit. It was built in 1642 on the orders of Christian IV, as part of a new university, to house a students' church, a library and, at the top, an

Rosenborg Castle stands in an expanse of glorious parkland and gardens ...

... best of all are the legions of tulips in the King's Gardens that give way to other blooms in summer

astronomical observatory. It still functions as an observatory, one of the oldest in Europe. A spiral walkway, over 200m long, was specially constructed round the tower to enable telescopes to be carried to the top.

The original church and library were destroyed by a fire in 1728, although the tower itself survived. Both have been reconstructed. Halfway up, a door leads into the library hall, which is now a venue for regularly changing exhibitions of art, culture, history and science. The baroque church is rather peaceful, missing out on the huge numbers of tourists who come only to climb the tower.

Købmagergade 52A (tel: 33 93 66 60). Open: September to May, 10am–5pm Monday to Saturday and noon–4pm Sunday; June to August 10am–8pm Monday to Saturday and noon–8pm Sunday. The Observatory is open October to March, 7–10pm Tuesday and Wednesday. Admission charge.

STATENS MUSEUM FOR KUNST (NATIONAL GALLERY)

Denmark's National Gallery has a rich collection of European and Danish paintings and sculpture, ranging from Byzantine icons through 17th-century European works to modern art.

The galleries, with their stately arches, ceilings and mosaic floors, are a fitting backdrop for the works of Dutch, Flemish and Italian masters displayed here, along with French Impressionists and 20th-century artists, including Rembrandt, Braque, Matisse and Picasso.

Of particular importance, however, is the extensive Danish collection, with examples of every major artist represented, from the Golden Age to the present.

Sølvgade 48–50 (tel: 33 91 21 26). Open: 10am–4.30pm Tuesday and Thursday to Sunday, plus 10am–9pm Wednesday. Admission charge.

THORVALDSENS MUSEUM

In 1838 the Copenhagen-born sculptor Bertel Thorvaldsen (1770–1844) presented his classical Greek and Roman-influenced works, plus his life-long collection of paintings and antiques, to his native city. A condition, however, was that a suitable building be found to house them. Consequently, an exquisite neoclassical house, with a mural-decorated façade, was erected to become the Thorvaldsens Museum.

It is well worth passing by simply to see the exterior; since entrance is free you will no doubt be tempted to wander among the statues, vases and paintings of the collection.

Porthusgade 2 (tel: 33 32 15 32). Open: 10am–5pm Tuesday to Sunday. Admission free.

TIVOLI GARDENS

Copenhagen's world-famous gardens lie at the heart of the city and are open for a fairytale celebration of fun and innocence throughout the summer. The gardens were founded in 1843, since when some 274 million people have wandered amid the thousands of blooms, the exuberant fountains, the ornamental lakes and the numerous amusements.

The Tivoli Gardens remain hugely popular with Danes and tourists of all ages, especially families. There are merry-go-rounds, roller-coasters, acrobats, musicians, dancers in fancy-dress, and troubadores acting out Hans Christian Andersen's stories. There are also numerous restaurants, cafés and bars.

After dark, over 100,000 lights of different colours illuminate the night sky. On Wednesdays, Fridays, Saturdays and Sundays, shortly before the clock strikes midnight, there is a magnificent explosion of fireworks. Then it is time to go home for bed, or alternatively to seek some of Copenhagen's less innocent nightlife.

Vesterbrogade 3 (tel: 33 15 10 01). Open: mid-April to mid-September, 10am–midnight daily. Admission charge.

Thorvaldsens Museum, backing on to a canal

One of an array of fanciful façades in Copenhagen's Tivoli Gardens, always enormously popular

VOR FRELSERS KIRKE (CHURCH OF OUR SAVIOUR)

The unusual spire of this church – pale greenish-blue, with an exterior spiral staircase and gilt railings – twists up to a summit crowned by a statue of Christ standing on top of a golden orb. The 400-step ascent is rewarded by a 360-degree panorama, and perhaps a bout of vertigo. The 17th-century church interior has a beautifully carved organ façade.

Prinsessegade/Skt Annæ Gade (tel: 31 57 27 98). Open: mid-March to end May and August to September, 9am–3.30pm Monday to Saturday and noon–1.30pm Sunday; June to August, 9am–4.30pm Monday to Saturday and noon–4.30pm Sunday; November to mid-March, 10am–1.30pm Monday to Saturday and noon–1.30pm Sunday. Admission to church free; admission charge to climb the spire.

VOR FRUE KIRKE (CHURCH OF OUR LADY)

Copenhagen's neoclassical cathedral stands in the heart of the Latin Quarter, opposite the main university building, and was reconstructed almost from scratch in the 19th century. Of the original building, which suffered two major disasters, only the walls of the side aisles and tower remain.

Even so, the cathedral is still worth a visit, if only to see Bertel Thorvaldsen's altar statues of Christ and the Twelve Apostles. The font, in the form of a shell held aloft by an angel, was also sculpted by Thorvaldsen.

Frue Plads (tel: 33 15 10 78). Open: 9am–5pm Monday to Saturday; in May to August, also noon–4.30pm Sunday: in September to April noon–1.30pm and 3–4.30pm Sunday. Admission free.

Copenhagen

This pilgrimage to the forgiveness-dispensing Little Mermaid starts in the centre of Copenhagen and weaves through the old town to the quayside. See map on pages 24–5.
Allow 2 hours.

Start on the Rådhuspladsen (Town Hall Square), hub of Copenhagen's bus network and effectively the centre of the city.

1 RÅDHUSET (TOWN HALL)

The huge rectangular town hall opened in 1903 and is where Copenhagen's political business is conducted. It is also one of the city's architectural jewels. A close look at the red-brick façade reveals countless details from Nordic mythology. The interior's main interests are Jens Olsen's extraordinary astronomical World Clock, and a climb up the tower for a great view of the city.

From the northeastern corner of the square, turn into pedestrianised Frederiksberggade. You are now on the 'Strøget'.

The Latin Quarter

2 STRØGET (THE PROMENADE)

The so-called 'Strøget' is a continuous pedestrianised walkway, some say the longest in the world, made up of five streets linking Rådhusplasen with Kongens Nytorv, Copenhagen's other main square. Along the route are both fashionable shops and tawdry boutiques, enlivened by legions of street entertainers. To the left is the Latin Quarter, so-called because it is the equivalent of the university district of Paris. Some way down is Gammel Torv Nytorv, the medieval marketplace alive with street traders once again.

Strøget spills into Kongens Nytorv (King's Square).

3 KONGENS NYTORV

Three imposing old buildings look out over this square, with its shady gardens, surrounded by cobbles laid in concentric

Town Hall Square

circles, like a running track. One is the old-fashioned Hotel d'Angleterre, the most prestigious place to stay in town, another is the honey-coloured, gilt-crested Kongelige Teater (Royal Theatre) and the third is the 17th-century Charlottenborg Palace, housing the handsome Royal Academy of Arts.

Continue across Kongens Nytorv and turn right along the furthest bank of the Nyhavn Canal.

4 NYHAVN CANAL

Traditional wooden schooners are moored along this Bohemian quayside, lined with pavement cafés. After dark there is a more raffish ambience, particularly among tattooing shops such as Danny and Bimbo's, at No 17.

Turn left onto Toldbodgade, roughly two thirds of the way down Nyhavn. Follow this street until it reaches the fountain, with the main docks to the right. Turn left into Amalienborg Plads (see pages 26–7) then right into Amaliegade, which brings you to the edge of Churchillparken.

5 FRIHEDSMUSEET (MUSEUM OF THE DANISH RESISTANCE)

This is the place to learn the story of the World War II Danish Resistance. News and other communications filtered through an underground press and munitions for sabotaging railways and factories, were received from Britain. The great act of heroism, however, was the national effort which helped thousands of Danish Jews escape to Sweden.

Walk through Churchillparken to the bridge across the moat that surrounds the Kastellet citadel, now a barracks. Continue straight through the Kastellet grounds and cross the moat again. Climb a staircase and turn right, heading for the crowd that has probably gathered around Copenhagen's smallest tourist attraction.

6 LILLE HAVFRUE (LITTLE MERMAID)

If you feel like confessing to excessive behaviour while in Copenhagen, here is the place to do it. This has been the role of the famous Little Mermaid ever since sailors discovered that such absolution made them feel a whole lot better (see page 32).

A walk back along the quayside, where ferries depart for Oslo, Malmö and Bornholm, brings you back to Nyhavn.

> **Resistance Museum**, (tel: 33 13 77 14). Open: May to mid-September Tuesday to Sunday, 10am–4pm; mid-September to April, Tuesday to Sunday 11am–3pm.

Copenhagen Harbour

This water tour is an excellent way to see Copenhagen from a perspective that, at times, is sharply different from land-based sightseeing. Tours are run by Canal Tours Copenhagen (tel: 33 13 31 05) between May and mid-September. *Allow about 1 hour.*

Tours start from Gammel Strand (and from Nyhavn).

1 GAMMEL STRAND

This was Copenhagen's most important quay in the Middle Ages. Until the 1950s it was also the site of a daily fish market, which explains the statue of a fishwife in traditional dress. The equestrian statue, further along the quay, is of Bishop Absalon, who effectively founded Copenhagen when he built the

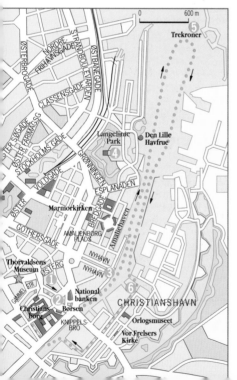

Christiansborg Palace on Slotsholmen Island (see page 30) across the canal. *The boats head for the open water and the Børsen building.*

2 BØRSEN (STOCK EXCHANGE)

The Dutch Renaissance Stock Exchange building is a typical creation of Christian IV's reign (1588–1648) when gracious mansions and public buildings were scattered throughout Copenhagen. The modern Copenhagen stock exchange has moved elsewhere.

To the left, as you leave the canal for the open harbour, is the Danish National Bank (Nationalbanken), a showpiece of modern architecture designed by the famous Danish architect, Arne Jacobsen.

3 NYHAVN

This is Denmark's best-known canal and the oldest part of the harbour. Its quay is lined with numerous bars, many of which evoke the days when the area was the haunt of sailors. Hans Christian

Canals reach into many corners of Copenhagen, and are an integral part of its charm

Andersen lived here during his two stays in Copenhagen, at numbers 18 (white) and 67 (red). The restored warehouse on the corner is a hotel and the lightship in front is a restaurant.

Back in the harbour are the Amaliehaven gardens to the left, with the Amalienborg Palace and Marmorkirken visible beyond.

4 LANGELINJE PARK
The most famous feature of the waterside Langelinje Park, to the left, is **Den Lille Havfrue** (The Little Mermaid, see page 32). The park's other monuments include the great Gefion fountain, inspired by the folk legend in which the Nordic Goddess Gefion was promised as much land as she could plough in a night; and the polar bear, recalling the days when Greenland was a Danish possession.

Here the boat continues to the Trekroner fortress, from where it returns to the harbour.

5 TREKRONER
The fortress, out in the harbour ahead, is built on an artificial island. It was used in 1801 in the battle commanded by Lord Nelson when Denmark became embroiled in the Napoleonic wars.

The boat leaves the harbour opposite the entrance to the Nyhavn canal, turning left to cruise along Christianshavn's canals.

6 CHRISTIANSHAVN
This district was established by King Christian IV in the 17th century as a separate town. Many of the gracious mansions and old warehouses lining the canal date from this period. Note the spire of Vor Frelsers Kirke (Church of Our Saviour – see page 41) rising above and on the left, the old naval hospital which houses the Orlogsmuseet (Naval Museum – see page 37).

The boat leaves the Christianshavn canal to cross the open harbour again. To the right is the Knippelsbro lifting bridge, connecting Slotsholmen with Christianshavn. You then return to Gammel Strand, passing the remains of the original Christiansborg Palace (see page 30) and the Thorvaldsens Museet (Thorvaldsens Museum see page 40), both on the right.

GREEN ETHICS

Even taking the most cursory glance at Denmark, there are signs that Danes are serious about environmental protection. In all Danish cities, for example, bicycles predominate as a means of transport; tracks are strictly for cyclists, who frequently have right of way over motor vehicles.

In the countryside, there is also plentiful evidence of pedal power on more than 5,000km of cycle paths. Much more stark indicators of the national commitment to alternative energy sources are the regiments of windmills (aerogenerators) which add an ultra-modern quality to the landscape, particularly on the flat and windy expanses of southern Jutland, or on the island of Bornholm.

Danish-designed 'Ellert' electric cars may offer a foretaste of future urban transport

Although unsightly to some, most Danes see these wind-powered generators as evidence that they are paying more than lip service to the green ethic. To date, wind power only generates a small fraction of the nation's electricity needs, but research on a serious scale continues apace to develop the technology to build large-scale generators. Tjæreborg, near Esbjerg, where a huge wind turbine dominates the surrounding landscape, is a major centre for this research.

Environmental policy is one of the chief criteria by which Danes judge their political parties. Any politically minded person you meet is likely to hold firm opinions, backed up by statistics, on the precise nature of

Jutland farmhouses and aerogenerators

the environmental threats that face the nation (if not the world) and the sort of policies needed to rectify them. Acid rain, toxic chemical waste dumps and excess greenhouse gases are all mainstream political issues.

On an everyday practical level, Danes tend to be uncommonly conscientious recyclers of bottles, paper, tin cans and anything else recyclable. Vegetables grown with organic fertilisers were widely available in Denmark long before they were in many other European countries. Likewise toiletries made only with natural ingredients and a host of other environmentally friendly goods are sought-after commodities.

Zealand (Sjælland)

*D*enmark's largest and most densely populated island is subject to the powerful magnetic pull of Copenhagen. It is quite possible to treat Zealand as an extensive suburb of the metropolis and visit most of its attractions in a few days based in the capital. North Zealand, in particular, has several awesome castles and historic towns all within less than an hour's ride of the city. Long sandy beaches, albeit crowded in summer, are also within easy reach.

But that's no way to get to know Zealand. To take a closer look at the island, it is important to keep away from Copenhagen for a while. Down in the south of Zealand a taste of rural, sleepy Denmark can be found. By the time you cross the bridge to the smaller islands off Zealand's southern tip, you will have just about escaped the city's orbit and can enjoy the relative remoteness and wilder scenery.

FALSTER

Linked by bridges to Zealand and Lolland, Falster Island is something of a thoroughfare. On the eastern side of the island, away from a steady stream of summer traffic (much of it travelling between Copenhagen and the ferries to and from Germany), there are some fine sandy beaches and rolling dunes. Naturists head for the beaches around **Bøtø** which are reserved for their naked delight.

Nykøbing F, the island's main town, hibernates from autumn to spring, becoming a lively holiday resort, with rows of open-air cafés, in the summer. The other attraction is **Czarens Hus** (Czar's House) where Peter the Great stayed in 1716.

Two bridges link Falster to southern Zealand, and a further three cross from Falster to Lolland (see page 53).

Bodies nearly ready for turning at Tisvildeleje Beach, North Zealand

ZEALAND

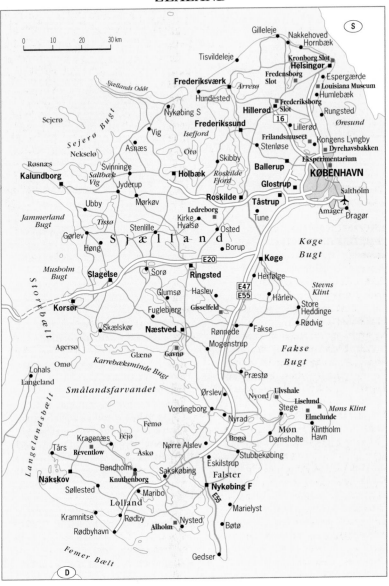

S

| 0 | 10 | 20 | 30 km |

Gilleleje
Nakkehoved
Hornbæk
Tisvildeleje
Kronborg Slot
Helsingør
Fredensborg
Slot
Espergærde
Frederiksværk
Arresø
Louisiana Museum
Humlebæk
Hundested
Frederiksborg
Slot
Sjællands Odde
Nykøbing S
Hillerød
16
Rungsted
Øresund
Sejerø
Frederikssund
Lillerød
Vig
Isefjord
Frilandsmuseet
Kongens Lyngby
Asnæs
Orø
Stenløse
Dyrehavsbakken
Nekselø
Svinninge
Skibby
Eksperimentarium
Røsnæs
Saltbæk
Vig
Holbæk
Roskilde
Fjord
Ballerup
KØBENHAVN
Kalundborg
Jyderup
Glostrup
Saltholm
Ubby
Mørkøv
Roskilde
Tåstrup
Amager
Dragør
_Jammerland
Bugt_
Tissø
Ledreborg
Tune
Stenlille
Kirke
Hvalsø
Osted
Gørlev
S j æ l l a n d
Borup
Køge
Bugt
Høng
E20
Køge
Musholm
Bugt
Slagelse
Sorø
Ringsted
Herfølge
Stevns
Klint
Glumsø
Haslev
E47
E55
Hårlev
Korsør
Fuglebjerg
Gisselfeld
Store
Heddinge
Skælskør
Næstved
Rødvig
Agersø
Rønnede
Fakse
Glænø
Gavnø
Mogenstrup
_Fakse
Bugt_
Omø
Karrebæksminde Bugt
Lohals
Præstø
Langeland
Smålandsfarvandet
Ørslev
Ulvshale
Nyord
Liselund
Vordingborg
Stege
Møns Klint
Femø
Nyrad
Elmelunde
Kragenæs
Fejø
Møn
Klintholm
Havn
Tårs
Reventlow
Askø
Nørre Alslev
Bogø
Damsholte
Bandholm
Stubbekøbing
Nakskov
Knuthenborg
Sakskøbing
Eskilstrup
Falster
Søllested
Maribo
Nykøbing F
Lolland
Marielyst
Kramnitse
Rødby
Nysted
Bøtø
Alholm
Rødbyhavn
Gedser
Femer Bælt

D

Frederiksborg Castle spans three islands stretched across the placid Castle Lake

FREDERIKSBORG SLOT (FREDERIKSBORG CASTLE)

Denmark's most magnificent Renaissance castle spans three small islands on the artificial Castle Lake, its spires, turrets, gables and copper-green roofs rising majestically above the town of Hillerød.

Much of the present structure was built by King Christian IV between 1602 and 1620. On ascending the throne he had the existing fortress, built by his father, Frederik II, in the previous half century, torn down. From 1671 to 1840 Frederiksborg was the Danish kings' home.

In the 18th-century a catastrophic series of fires virtually razed Hillerød to the ground, destroying much of the castle. Under the patronage of J C Jacobsen, the owner of Carlsberg Breweries, a massive restoration programme was initiated. The result was a masterful reconstruction of the damaged sections, which are almost impossible to distinguish from the original parts.

The two highlights of the castle tour include the gilded **Ridder Kapellet** (Coronation Chapel), where monarchs were crowned during the two centuries when it was a royal palace, and the cavernous **Riddersalen** (Knights' Hall) with its amazingly embellished high-vaulted ceiling.

Since 1878 the castle has been Denmark's **Nationalhistoriske Museum** (Museum of National History), housing a vast collection of historical paintings, portraits, wall-sized tapestries, furniture and other antiques, displayed in endless glittering halls, chambers and corridors of gilt, crystal, marble and carved wood panelling.

There are superb views of the highly photogenic castle and its reflection in the water, from the gardens on the far side of the lake.

Frederiksborg Slot is at 3400 Hillerød, 30km north of Copenhagen (tel: 42 26 04 39). Open: May to September, 10am–5pm daily; April and October, 10am–4pm, daily; November to March, 11am–3pm daily. Admission charge.

FRILANDSMUSEET

This open-air museum, set in a beautiful wooded landscape, illustrates rural life in the 17th, 18th and 19th centuries. The museum contains about 100 faithfully reconstructed buildings, some of them dismantled and reassembled stone by stone from all over Denmark. Many of the buildings are set in their authentic re-created environs. The coastal farm, for example, is surrounded by sand dunes and marram grass; the watermill is next to a stream. Inside are original furniture, tools and ornaments.

The Frilandsmuseet justifies a visit of several hours, as you can follow a course through the park, building up a picture of the diversity of Danish country life in different ages, regions and social classes.

The Frilandsmuseet is at 100 Kongevejen in Kongens Lyngby, 13km north of Copenhagen (tel: 45 85 02 92). Open: 26 April to end September; 10am–5pm Tuesday to Sunday; 1 to 14 October 10am–3pm Tuesday to Friday and noon–5pm Saturday and Sunday; 15 to 23 October, 10am–4pm daily. Admission charge.

GILLELEJE

Gilleleje, at Zealand's northern tip, dates from around 1500 and is one of Denmark's oldest fishing ports. The harbour is alive year-round with light-blue fishing boats whose catches are frequently auctioned on the quayside. In summer this is also a humming tourist town with open-air bars and beaches nearby. A footpath leading out of town up on to the dunes makes a good walk.

The town has a small museum of local fishing and natural history, which is worth a quick visit. About 2km east, at **Nakkehoved**, is the world's first coal-fired lighthouse, built in 1772, now a small museum.

Gilleleje Museum is 60km north of Copenhagen. The tourist office is at Hovedgade 6F (tel: 48 30 01 74). Gilleleje Museum, 2 Rostgårdsvej (tel: 48 30 16 31). Admission charge includes entry to the Nakkehoved lighthouse. Both open: mid-June to mid-September, 2–5pm daily.

Fishing boats and pleasure craft moored alongside each other in Gilleleje's harbour

The floor of Kronborg Castle's Great Hall reflects a chequered history

HELSINGØR (ELSINORE)

Helsingør is a frontier town, facing Sweden across the Øresund. This is one of the world's busiest seaways, adding a constant commotion to the old commercial port. This grew prosperous on the 'Sound Dues' payed by every vessel which passed through between 1427 and 1857: '400 years of legal piracy' claimed some; 'The Danish King's golden egg' said the more sympathetic.

The town's reputation, however, has been largely hijacked by Hamlet, William Shakespeare's not-quite-fictitious Prince of Denmark. He was probably named after a mythological Viking figure known as Amleth. Appropriately enough Kronborg Castle, where most of the action of the world's most famous drama takes place, is the town's most dominant feature.

Helsingør is 50km north of Copenhagen. The tourist office is at Havnepladsen 3, Box 60 (tel: 49 21 13 33).

Kronborg Slot (Kronenburg Castle)

The 16th-century, four-winged Renaissance castle, built on the site of an older fortress overlooking the strategic Øresund, has been restored as a **historical museum**. Many visitors like to take a walk round the outer wall, cogitating on whether to be or not to be, before paying to go inside and explore the King's and Queen's chambers, richly ornamented with extravagant doorways, marble fireplaces, Flemish tapestries and ceiling paintings. The bare Great Hall is claimed to be Europe's longest room at 62m.

The castle also houses a separate **Handels-og Søfartsmuseet på** (Trade and Maritime Museum), charting the history of Denmark's trade and shipping through the ages.

Kronborg Slot (tel: 49 21 06 85). Open: May to September, 10.30am–5pm daily; April and October, 11am–4pm Tuesday to Sunday; November to March, 11am–3pm Tuesday to Sunday. Admission charge.

Handels-og Søfartsmuseet (tel: 49 21 06 85). Open: same hours as castle. Additional admission charge.

HORNBÆK

This pretty fishing port is located near some superb beaches on the northern coast, looking across the Øresund to Kullen on a promontory jutting out of Sweden. A 200-berth marina has made it a favourite of the yachting community. It is also the starting point for the annual round-Zealand regatta in June.

Hornbæk is 12km west of Helsingør. The tourist office is at Vestre Stejlebakke 2A (tel: 49 70 47 47).

KALUNDBORG

This is the place to catch a ferry to Århus in Jutland, or to the island of Samsø. It is also worth walking round the town's small, medieval kernel, to see the 12th-century **Vor Frue Kirke** (Church of Our Lady) with its five-towered spire; almost uniquely in Denmark, the church is

shaped as a Greek cross. Away from the centre is the medieval **Gamle Tiendelade** (Old Tithe Barn) and the small **Kalundborg og Omegns** (Museum of Kalundborg's Surroundings).

Kalundborg is 103km west of Copenhagen. The tourist office is at Volden 12 (tel: 53 51 09 15).

Many of Lolland Island's cottages are thatched

LOLLAND ISLAND

Denmark's third largest island (after Zealand and Funen) is flat and sparsely populated, with great expanses of beach and an interior of extensive farmland and woods. It is linked to Falster and thence to Zealand by road, and to Germany via a ferry across the Femer Bælt. Many visitors simply pass through, finding little to detain them on the island. Those with time on their hands should stop at Maribo and see the 15th-century **cathedral** with its brilliant white interior and gilt altarpiece.

Lolland, south of Zealand, is linked to Falster by three road bridges (see page 48).

LOUISIANA, MUSEUM FOR MODERNE KUNST (MUSEUM OF MODERN ART)

A giant Henry Moore welcomes visitors to this collection of galleries set amidst landscaped parkland strewn with sculptures and huge trees, leading down to the Øresund.

The museum is internationally famous for its travelling art exhibitions, films and concerts with an ever-changing list of events. Represented in the permanent exhibitions are sculptures by Alexander Calder, Jean Arp, Max Ernst, and Alberto Giacometti, as well as Henry Moore; and paintings by Picasso and Warhol, as well as by prominent Danes, including Richard Mortensen, Asger Jorn, Robert Jacobsen and Carl H Petersen.

Gl Strandvej 13, Humlebæk, on the Copenhagen to Helsingør coastal road,

Thumbs up at the Louisiana Museum

35km north of the capital (tel: 42 19 07 19). Open: 10am–5pm Monday, Tuesday, Thursday and Friday; 10am–10pm Wednesday; 10am–6pm Saturday and Sunday. Admission charge.

MØN

Møn is by far the most beautiful of the islands south of Zealand, with its rolling green hills and its spectacular white chalk sea cliffs at Møns Klint. As the nearest thing Denmark has to dramatic scenery, these cliffs draw crowds year round. From a huge car park, trails plunge into dense woodland and along the roller-coaster cliff. It is possible to scramble down to the beach below, although following the recent death of a tourist in a landslide, caution is called for.

Møn is linked by road bridge to mainland Zealand, and to Falster via the tiny island of Bogø. There is a tourist office in Stege, Møn's main town, at Storegade 2, (tel: 55 81 44 11).

The cliffs at Møn are as white as blackboard chalk

NÆSTVED

Næstved grew up around a Benedictine monastery which now houses the Herlufen, Denmark's most famous boarding school. Later it was a Hanseatic trading port and today it is the largest town in south Zealand. It is also a garrison town and home to the Gardehussar regiment (Hussars of the Household Cavalry) who ride through the town centre amid colourful fanfare every Wednesday morning.

At other times the town has a rather sleepy air, though there are several points of interest. Næstved has two superb Gothic churches – **St Morten's**, best known for its massive altarpiece, while St Peter's has some richly decorated frescos.

Næstved Museum is housed in the Helligåndshuset (House of the Holy Spirit), a charitable institution dating from about 1400 with a good collection of medieval and modern wood carvings.

Næstved is 80km southwest of Copenhagen. The tourist office is at Det Gule Pakhus, Havnen 1 (tel: 53 72 11 22).

RINGSTED

A natural crossroads in the centre of Zealand, Ringsted has a rich history as an important settlement in Viking times, and subsequently as a medieval ecclesiastical centre. Today roads still converge on the town from all corners of the island, but its significance is mainly as an agricultural hub.

With much recent building (including shopping precincts and a new town hall), Ringsted gives the overall impression of a modern town. However, dominating the whole is the sturdy **Sankt Bendts Kirke** (Saint Bendt's Church), begun in 1160 by Valdemar the Great to house the shrine to his revered father, Knud Lavard. The shrine became a pilgrimage destination and was the burial site for Danish kings until the 14th century.

The royal tombs are the focus of the church; it is well worth visiting at a quiet time when the atmosphere is intensified. Particularly striking are the brass and alabaster burial slabs of Erik Menved and his wife, Queen Ingeborg.

Ringsted is 28km north of Næstved. The tourist office is at Sankt Bendtsgade 10 (tel: 53 61 34 00).

The Viking Ship Museum is a good place to feel the spirit of ancient Norsemen

ROSKILDE

Roskilde grew into a prominent town in Viking times, its position on the Roskilde fjord giving access to the open sea. In the 12th century Bishop Absalon made it the headquarters of the Danish church, founding the cathedral here, and hence effectively the national capital. It remained so until 1400 when the court moved to Copenhagen. Danish monarchs are still buried here.

Apart from the annual July Roskilde Festival weekend, one of Europe's largest rock-music events, most visitors come to Roskilde to visit the cathedral.

Vikingeskibshallen (Viking Ship Museum)

Situated down below the town at the edge of the Roskilde Fjord. On display are the carefully reconstructed remains of five Viking long boats discovered and excavated between 1962 and 1967.

Viking Ship Museum (tel: 42 80 63 63).

Open: April to October, 9am–5pm; September to March, 10am–5pm.

Roskilde is 30km west of Copenhagen. The tourist office is at Gullandsstræde 15 (tel: 42 35 27 00).

Domkirke (Cathedral)

The massive red-brick cathedral is one of the most impressive buildings in Denmark. It is also one of the most architecturally important, with extensions in different styles added over the centuries. Work started in the 1170s on the orders of Bishop Absalon, though the main structure, a mixture of Gothic and Romanesque, was not finished until the early 1400s. The tall, thin, highly characteristic steeples were added in the 16th century.

The interior is vast, airy and adorned with innumerable treasures and historical curiosities. Don't miss the ingenious 16th-century clock on the south wall, just above the entrance, where a

mechanical St George attacks a dragon on the hour.

The main sights, however, are the royal tombs where 20 kings and 17 queens are interred in four chapels. There is a great variety of styles amid the gilt, marble, silver and bronze – ranging from the richly ornamented chapel of Christian IV, to the simple slab marking the resting place of Frederik IX, father of the present queen.

10 Domkirkestræde (tel: 42 35 16 24). Open: May to October, 9am–4.45pm Monday to Saturday and 12.30–3.45pm Sunday; September and April, 9am–4.45pm Monday to Friday, 11.30am–4.45pm Saturday and 12.30–3.45pm Sunday; October to March, 10am–2.45pm Monday to Friday, 11.30am–2.45pm Saturday and 12.30–3.45pm Sunday. In July and August there are guided tours in English at 11.30am Monday to Saturday, and at 2pm on Sunday. Admission charge.

RUNGSTED

The Karen Blixen Museet (Museum), dedicated to the life of the novelist and traveller (1885–1962), is the reason to stop at Rungsted. The large country house was her childhood home and is where she returned in 1931 to write *Out of Africa* and other works. She died here in 1962 and is buried in a movingly simple grave under a beech tree in the grounds.

A tour of the house takes in the rooms where Blixen lived and wrote. There is also an exhibition of photographs spanning her life, including many taken in Africa, plus a 16ha park which is now a bird sanctuary.

Rungsted is on the 152N coastal road, 20km south of Helsingør. Karen Blixen Museet, Strandvej 111, Rungsted Kyst (tel: 42 57 10 57). Open: May to September 10am–5pm daily; October to April, 1–4pm Wednesday to Sunday. Admission charge.

VORDINGBORG

Vordingborg is an old market town and port, much of which has been rebuilt in recent years, giving it a modern aspect. Linked by bridge to Møn, many motorists pass through the town on their way to the island. The main attraction is the **Gasetårn** (Goose Tower), the only surviving corner of a 14th-century wall which once surrounded a massive castle, now in ruins. The tower, supposedly once crowned by a gilded goose as a calculated insult to Hanseatic traders, can be climbed for commanding views over the town and across to Møn.

Vordingborg is at the southwestern tip of Zealand, opposite the island of Falster. The tourist office is at Glambæksvej 3 (tel: 54 13 62 98).

North Zealand

This car tour winds a leisurely way along some of North Zealand's minor roads and winding lanes, crossing humpback bridges and tracing the shores of lakes and fjords. Much of it is on the 'Marguerite Route' (for details of which see Driving on pages 182–3), and it skirts several major attractions described elsewhere in this section. *Allow about 5 hours.*

From central Copenhagen follow signs for the 152N coastal road, which is also signposted as the Marguerite Route. Just past the up-market suburb of Charlottenlund the metropolis ends, with Bellevue beach on the right and the Dyrehave, at Klampenborg, on the left.

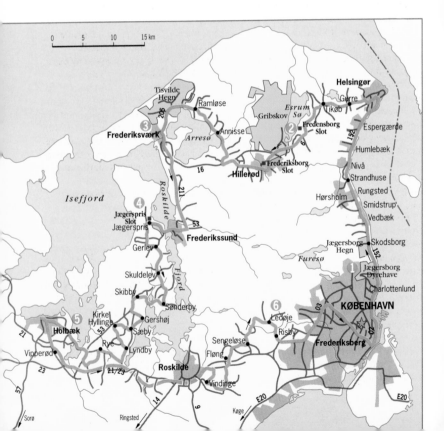

1 JÆGERSBORG DYREHAVE

Denmark's oldest deer park has been preserved as an expanse of open land and broad leafed forest, covering more than 1,000 undulating hectares. It is a glorious place to stretch the legs or, for the less energetic, to spot deer from the horse-drawn carriages that are for hire.

Continue north along the 152. As you reach Helsingør (see page 52), take the Marguerite Route left towards Hillerød, stopping at Fredensborg Slot (castle).

2 FREDENSBORG SLOT

Often known as 'The Palace of Peace', this summer residence of the Danish royal family is spectacularly set on the edge of Esrum Sø (lake). Completed in 1776, its style is more that of a country house than a defensive castle. Parts of the palace are open to the public at restricted times in summer, but the real treat is to wander the lakeside gardens, open all year.

Continue along the Marguerite Route, passing Hillerød (see page 50) to the left, before curving round the northern end of Arresø (lake) to Frederiksværk.

3 FREDERIKSVÆRK

It is worth stopping at the town to walk along the canal towpath connecting Arresø lake (Denmark's largest) with the Roskilde Fjord which leads to the open sea. The town grew up around this canal.

The Marguerite Route traces the eastern side of the boat-dotted Roskilde Fjord, with farmland and paddocked horses to the right. At Frederikssund turn right for the bridge over the fjord, following the route round to Jægerspris Slot.

4 JÆGERSPRIS SLOT

This superb castle, set in fine gardens, probably dates back to the 11th century, but was completely rebuilt by Frederik VII who acquired it in 1854 and died there in 1863.

Continue along the Marguerite Route, twisting through hidden backwaters and medieval villages away from the main road, as far as Holbæk.

5 HOLBÆK

Fjord-side Holbæk is one of the most ancient towns in Zealand, starting first as a port and later becoming the seat of a Dominican priory. While exploring the fascinating back streets and half-timbered houses, do not miss the excellent museum illustrating the development of the town and surrounding area.

Join the main 21 road eastwards towards Roskilde (see page 56) rejoining the Marguerite Route immediately east of the town. Follow the route to Ledøje.

6 LEDØJE

This small village has one of the most unusual churches in Denmark. Built with two storeys, one for commoners and one for the gentry, the 13th-century building is effectively two churches sharing a single altar.

Follow the Marguerite Route back into central Copenhagen.

Jægerspris Slot (tel: 47 53 10 04). Open: May to September, 10am–noon and 1–5pm Tuesday to Saturday; April to October, same times but Sunday only.

Museet for Holbæk og Omegn, Klosterstræde. Open: 10am–4pm Tuesday to Sunday.

Bornholm

*T*his small island out in the Baltic, 180km east of Zealand, has become one of Denmark's most popular tourist resorts. Expanses of beach, dramatically rocky headlands, formidable ruined castles, rolling pastures, fairytale woodland, whitewashed churches, huddled harbours and quaint, gaily painted villages of half-timbered cottages, all help to make it irresistible to the lover of peace and tranquillity.

BORNHOLM

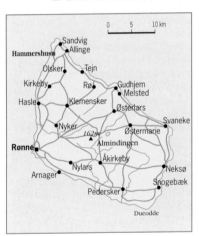

For the cyclist, there are more than 200km of winding paths to explore, making it a joy for relaxed pedal power. Peace in this idyll has not been easily won, however. Its strategic position in the Baltic has led to Bornholm being fought over for centuries, most recently in 1945 when the commandant of the occupying Germans refused to surrender following capitulation to the allies. The Russians responded by bombing Rønne and Neksø, the two main towns, and themselves occupying the island for several months before returning it to Danish sovereignty. Bornholm then spent the Cold War as one of

Nato's key surveillance bases.

Islanders have a strong desire that their hard-fought way of life should not be diluted by unfettered tourism. Consequently there are special laws that help keep the island communities alive; including one forbidding any foreigner from buying land in Denmark and others restricting the use of homes as holiday properties. Another measure is the strict monitoring of air and ferry tickets, ensuring that the total number of visitors never more than doubles the resident population of around 45,000.

ÅKIRKEBY See page 65.

CHRISTIANSØ
From Gudhjem, Svaneke or Allinge (near the north tip of Bornholm) you can take a ferry across about 17km of water to Christiansø, the largest in a tiny archipelago of Danish specks in the Baltic. Together with Frederiksø, the other inhabited island, Christiansø supports a population of about 130. A third, Græsholm, is a protected bird sanctuary.

The islands were fortified by Christian V and played an important role in the Napoleonic wars, when attacks on the British fleet were launched from here. They now make an interesting day-trip.

Christiansø lies 20km to the east of Bornholm island.

Gudhjem: smoked herring drying and one of the town's two little harbours (inset)

DUEODDE

Dueodde is Bornholm's number one beach area, with rolling dunes and endless stretches of sand so fine that, in bygone days, it used to be exported all over Europe as 'writing sand' to sprinkle over and absorb wet ink. The beach shelves so gently into the sea that, in places, the tide comes in and out as fast as you can walk. In the opposite direction, the dunes lead into sandy pine woodlands dotted with holiday cottages. There are also several camp sites.

There is no village to Dueodde – just a hotel, café and bus stop, plus a lighthouse which opens to the public at irregular times.

Dueodde is 20km southeast of Rønne.

GUDHJEM

So steep is the main street leading down from a rocky headland to Gudhjem that cyclists are required to dismount by law. Fig trees and vines, climbing up the red-tiled cottages huddled round the two harbours, lend the little port a Mediterranean mien. Movie buffs might recognise the place as one of the settings for the Oscar-winning *Pelle the Conqueror,* based on Martin Andersen Nexø's novel about the miserable life of Swedish immigrants on Bornholm in the 19th century.

Today, Gudhjem is best known for its herring smokehouses. Here you can watch fresh fish being gutted, dried in the wind and hung in a chimney while

men use damp sacking on the end of sticks to beat the flames down, keeping the smoke billowing. It is thought by some that this technique was taught to Gudhjem fishermen by Scottish soldiers stationed on Christiansø. Whatever the truth, a visit to Gudhjem should be rounded off with a meal of these 'Golden Bornholmers', still warm from the smokery; they are delicious served with black rye bread, course sea salt and strong Danish beer.

There is a small museum in the abandoned railway station, worth a visit to see the collection of local art.

Gudhjem is 19km northeast of Rønne. The tourist office is at Åbogade 9 (tel: 56 48 52 10).

Museum. Open: mid-May to mid-September, 10am–4pm Monday to Saturday, and 2–5pm Sunday.

HAMMERSHUS

The massive, ruined castle of Hammershus perches dramatically at the edge of the island's 75m high north-western cliff. Historians disagree about the castle's origins, though few dispute that it was once the greatest fortress in northern Europe. It was probably built in the 13th century, during the struggle between the Danish Crown and Church. With the defence of Bornholm so vital to control of the Baltic, it changed hands many times, and was expanded by many rulers, before being severely damaged by artillery when Bornholm was captured by Sweden in 1645. Thirteen years later the people of Bornholm revolted against the Swedes and the castle was never again used as a fortress. It later became a prison, then a garrison, before falling into disrepair.

The best way to sense the overall scale of the castle is to walk all the way round the ring wall that encircles it. A bridge from the eastern side gives access to the castle ruins themselves.

Hammershus is 20km north of Rønne. There is unrestricted access to the castle ruins all year round.

MELSTED

Tiny Melsted is worth a visit for the agricultural museum housed in the 17th-century Melstedgård farm. This is a 'living museum' where the traditional agricultural methods of the island are demonstrated in action. There are also various exhibits on farming life through the ages, with tableaux and original implements.

Melsted is 1km south of Gudhjem, 18km northeast of Rønne. Melstedgård Agricultural Museum, Melstedvej 25 (tel: 56 48 55 98). Open: mid-May to mid-September, 10am–5pm Tuesday to Sunday.

Left: the ruins of Hammershus Castle
Below: Melstedgård Agricultural Museum

Bornholm's round churches also served as strongholds and observation posts

NEKSØ

Neksø, on Bornholm's east coast, is the island's second largest town, although the population is barely 4,000. The harbour, however, is out of all proportion to the rest of the port, busy with the constant toing and froing of fishing boats and with the cry of seabirds filling the air. Although Neksø was bombed by the Russians in 1945, parts of the old centre, characterised by sandstone-walled houses, have survived.

Neksø is 25km east of Rønne. The Neksø-Dueodde tourist office is at Åsen 4 (tel: 56 49 32 00).

ØSTERLARS

The thickset circular church at Østerlars is the largest and best known of several on Bornholm built not just as places of worship, but also as look-out posts and a last line of defence for villagers against whatever enemies might be lurking offshore. Seven massive buttresses support the walls, rising three storeys high, which can be climbed via narrow interior staircases. Through narrow slit windows there are commanding views over the island and the grey sea beyond the shores.

Østelars is 17km northeast of Rønne. Østelars Kirke, Gudjemsvej 28. Open: April to October, 9am–5pm Monday to Saturday. Admission charge.

RØNNE

With a population of about 15,000, Rønne is Bornholm's main town and capital. The 1945 Russian bombing left few parts of the town intact, but many of the narrow streets of cross-timbered houses, painted bright yellow, orange and blue, have been carefully rebuilt, contributing to the atmosphere of an oversized village.

There is a large harbour where fishing boats and ferries to Copenhagen, Sweden, Germany and Poland dock. The town also has a yachting marina and, near by, some good beaches.

Rønne's tourist office, which is also the main one for the island, is the Bornholms Velkomstcenter, Ndr Kystvej 3 (tel: 56 95 95 00).

Bornholm Museum

This is the place to delve into the history and prehistory of Bornholm. Among the finds is a collection of Roman gold and silver coins unearthed on the island. There are also some beautiful paintings by Bornholmer artists, capturing the light and essence of the island, and displays of ceramics by several of the island's famous potters.

Sankt Mortensgade 29 (tel: 56 95 07 35). Open: April to October, 10am–5pm Monday to Saturday and 1–5pm Sunday; November to March, 2–5pm Tuesday, Thursday and Sunday. Admission charge.

SVANEKE

This picturesque little port of 1,200 souls nestles in a cove on the island's rocky north-eastern coast, bringing a splash of colour with its bright, limewashed and half-timbered houses. It is also one of the smallest market towns in Denmark, with a charter dating back more than 400 years. The whole village has been a conservation area since 1968. In 1975 – European Building Preservation Year – it was awarded the European Council's prize for preserving historical character.

Svaneke is 20km east of Rønne. The tourist office is at Storegade 24 (tel: 56 49 63 50).

Sleepy Åkirkeby was once Bornholm's key town

ÅKIRKEBY

In the Middle Ages when pirates and other enemies at sea kept population centres away from the coast, this inland town was the most important on Bornholm, with the island's regional council meeting here until 1776.

It was also the ecclesiastical centre, with the island's most unusual church; its thickest 12th-century walls suggest that, like many other Bornholmer churches, it also served a defensive purpose. There is a fine late-Romanesque porch, decorated with rune stones, and a superb baptismal font carved from stone.

Åkirkeby is 12km east of Rønne. The tourist office is at Torvet 2 (tel: 56 97 45 20).

Bornholm by Bike

This ride through Bornholm's undulating interior takes in the island's beautiful scenery, as well as some unexpected surprises along the way.
Allow 3 hours.

1 RØNNE

Bikes are the main form of transport in the town, with cycle tracks lining all the main streets (see page 64). Islanders and holidaymakers can be seen on an extraordinary variety of two-wheeled contraptions, going about their business with bells ringing, or setting off for a day in the countryside.

Take the signposted cycle track towards Lobbæk, which follows the bed of the disused Rønne to Neksø railway line. After about 4km, stop at the village of Nylars, where the traditional round church can be seen on the left.

2 NYLARS RUNDKIRKE (NYLARS ROUND CHURCH)

This is a perfect example of the round, white-walled churches that are sprinkled around Bornholm. Like several others on the island, it was built in the troublesome 12th century and was as much a defensive bastion as a place of worship. In 1335 it was dedicated to the patron saint of seafarers, St Nicholas. Note the circular central pillar, decorated with a frieze.

Continue to the village of Lobbæk. Here you leave the former railway, but stay on the cycle track that continues through fields dotted with aerogenerators, then follows the metalled road from Rønne to Åkirkeby. About 5km on from Lobbæk, you spill into Åkirkeby.

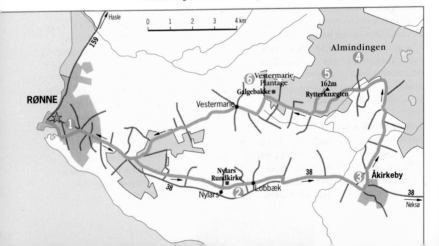

3 ÅKIRKEBY

See page 65.

Follow the signposted cycle track north from the village, towards Almindingen and Gudhjem. You soon plunge into forest.

4 ALMINDINGEN

Almindingen, meaning 'The Common', is the third largest forest in Denmark – covering 24sq km of the island's hilliest ground. It was cleared in the 17th century as a public grazing area for cattle, but later replanted with a mixture of deciduous and coniferous trees. This is the most enchanting part of the day's ride, as the path meanders past marshy ponds alive with noisily croaking frogs.

Follow a signpost to the right, which leads steadily up a track to Rytterknægten, an iron-girder tower rising out of the forest.

5 RYTTERKNÆGTEN

The tower marks the highest point on the island, and the third highest in the whole of Denmark. Climbing up the tower provides an unexpected reminder of Bornholm's strategic location between the east and the west. As you leave the treetops behind, an array of aerials, dishes, receivers and all kinds of surveillance equipment emerges from leafy hiding places. A stark sign warns you not to take photographs.

Return to the main Rønne–Gudhjem cycle track and follow it towards Rønne, stopping after 1.5km at the Vestermarie Plantage.

6 VESTERMARIE PLANTAGE (PLANTATION)

This is one of the most interesting archaeological sites on Bornholm, with several points of interest within a very short distance of each other. Just south of the cycle track are some fine Bronze Age carved-stone ships; near by is a distinctive mound, known as Galgebakke, believed to have been a place of execution. Beside the mound is a dense collection of cairns, marking the burial site of urns containing cremated human remains.

Continue along the cycle track back towards Rønne. Shortly before the town, it rejoins the Rønne-Åkirkeby track along the disused railway.

THE GREAT BELT AND

Two civil engineering projects, each among the most ambitious the world has ever seen, are due to come to fruition before the millennium. Together they will link Copenhagen and the Island of Zealand, via Funen, to the Jutland peninsula and to the Swedish mainland.

The Great Belt Fixed Link, due to open at the end of the 1990s, spans 18km of sea by means of two bridges and a bored tunnel. Between them they will carry a four-lane motorway and two railway tracks, one for each direction. The West Bridge, Europe's longest combined road and railway bridge at 6.6km, goes across to the island of

Below: the East Tunnel
Right: the 6.6km West Bridge to the island of Spogø was completed in 1995
Far right: the world's longest suspension bridge, currently under construction, will complete the Great Belt project

ØRESUND PROJECTS

Sprogø. Road and railway then divide, with the 6.8km East Bridge, the world's longest offshore suspension bridge, carrying the motor traffic. The railway dives into an 8km tunnel, the breakthrough of which was completed in October 1994.

The even more ambitious Øresund Fixed Link, due to open in 1997, spans the 16km divide between Denmark and Sweden. Like the Great Belt link, it will carry a four-lane motorway and two railway tracks. The plan is for a 7.5km

bridge from the Swedish coast to connect with two artificial islands. From these, the fixed link will pass into a 3.8km immersed tunnel under the Drogden channel.

There are Visitor Centres on both sides of the Great Belt Fixed Link, at Knudshoved Færgehavn, in Nyborg on Funen, and at Storeboeltsvej 88, in Korsor on Zealand (tel for both: 58 35 01 00). The Øresund Fixed Link Visitor Centre is at Kastrup Strandpark 9, Kastrup, Zealand.

Funen (Fyn)

*G*reen as a croquet lawn, the country's second largest island is often called the 'Garden of Denmark'. The term is thought to have been used first by Hans Christian Andersen. Funen's gently rolling hills, luxuriant pastures, broad-leaved forests and winding lanes were a source of inspiration to the great poet and author of many well-loved fairy stories.

The same notions of flowing magical beauty are to be found in the works of fellow islander Carl Nielsen, Denmark's foremost composer. He is said to have believed that the lilting local accent was an expression of a rare musicality among the people of Funen.

Funen is joined to Jutland by a bridge spanning the Lillebælt. When the Great Belt Fixed Link to Zealand is completed (see page 68), virtually everybody will arrive by land. Even so, there is little danger of Funen losing its insularity.

Odense, the main city, gives the impression of an oversized village, despite its numerous cultural riches. There are beaches, fishing villages and coves dotted around the coast. Inland, fields of wheat and vegetables are sprinkled with farmhouses, windmills, whitewashed churches and the occasional castle or grand old manor. The land becomes more undulating to the south, but seldom too steep for cycling on Funen's bike-friendly roads.

To the south is an archipelago of smaller islands reached from the port of Svendborg, with an even stronger aura of calm and isolation. Langeland and Ærø, in particular, are excellent for cycling.

ÆRØ

By far the largest of Funen's islands not to be connected by bridge, Ærø is the jewel of the archipelago. Holidaymakers boarding ferries from Svendborg or Fåborg are lured by the gentle green hills topped with windmills and strewn with prehistoric burial mounds, as well as the abundant bird life, the beaches, the idyllic fishing ports and the farming hamlets. Few bother to bring their cars – Ærø is ideal hiking and biking country.

Ærø is 12km south of Fåborg.

Ærøskøbing

Impossibly pretty, the romantic town of Ærøskøbing, on Aerø, consists of half-timbered cottages, some of them charmingly higgledy-piggledy and lime washed in a spectrum of colours, interspersed with larger bow-windowed houses.

The squares and cobbled alleys are littered with curiosities, such as ancient wooden water pumps, and the oldest post office in Denmark (dating from 1749). You may feel you are in a giant museum already, but there are several more scattered about town, including the **Ærø Museum** on Brogade 3–5 (tel: 62 52 29 50) which charts the history of the island, and the **Flaskeskibssamlingen** with a vast collection of bottle-ships at Smedgade 22 (tel: 62 52 29 51).

Ærøskøbing is on the northern coast of Ærø.

ASSENS

Assens is an enchanting little fishing port, yachting centre and holiday town on the Lillebælt. It comprises an old town of gabled merchants' houses and a busy modern shopping centre.

The chief attraction is **'De 7 Haver'**, seven gardens laid out in contrasting styles to represent the horticultural traditions of different European nations.

Assens is 39km southwest of Odense. Idéhaven 'De 7 Haver', Aa-Strandvej 60–62, Ebberup (tel: 65 74 12 85). Open: April to November, 10am–5pm daily. Admission charge.

FUNEN

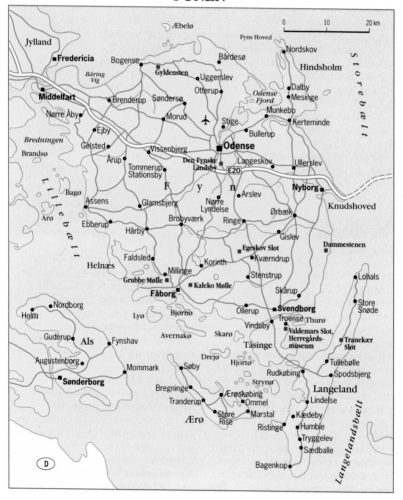

Dreamlike Egeskov Castle looks as if it has come straight out of a fairytale

EGESKOV SLOT (EGESKOV CASTLE)

Standing in the middle of a lake, like a giant ship at anchor, this soaring and surrealistically pink turreted castle is one of Denmark's most famous landmarks. It is a rare example of a Danish national monument in the private ownership of an aristocratic family. In some ways its massive solid proportions sit uneasily with the surrounding understated landscape, but no visit to Funen is complete without seeing Egeskov.

Visitors cross a drawbridge to reach the interior, where the rooms are themed on different eras in the castle's 440-year history. White walls give it an airy feel as you wander, alone or with an optional guide, from the Louis XVI Gule Stue (Yellow Room) to the 19th-century Klunkestuen (Victorian Room) and through many other chambers exquisitely furnished with period pieces. Most striking are the Jagtstuen (Hunting Room) and Jagtgangen (Hunting Corridor) hung with thousands of African big-game trophies shot by a former owner earlier this century.

Peacocks strut and flags flutter in the surrounding gardens where a veteran motor museum, with a fine collection of carriages, cars, motorcycles and aircraft, fills various outhouses. There is also a maze and a large children's playground.

Egeskov Slot is 27km south of Odense, at Egeskovgade 18 Kværndrup (tel: 62 27 10 74). Open: May and September, 10am–5pm daily; June to August, 9am–6pm daily (castle 10am–5pm). Admission charge.

FÅBORG

Looking out across the sea from southwestern Funen to some of the smallest islands of the archipelago, this delightful little port is a ferry hub with connections to Ærø, Als and Gelting (in Germany), and to tiny Lyø, Avernakø and Bjørnø.

A busy waterfront road hides a maze of back alleys, archways, cobbles and photogenic streets, particularly Tårngade, lined with old merchants' houses and hung with flowers. On the hour, a carillon chimes hymn tunes from the belfry high above.

Fåborg Museum

This is the place to view the works of the famous 'Funen Painters' school of landscape artists, which flourished from 1890 to 1920. Peter Hansen, Fritz Syberg and Johannes Larsen were the leading lights of the era, and this is the most extensive collection anywhere of their work. Those who have already slowed down to the gentle pace of Funen's rural life, noticing its bright colours and feeling the breeze rustling in the oak forests, will appreciate how superbly this trio capture the island's atmosphere.

Also on display is the work of local sculptors, including the renowned Kai Nielsen, and some Funen furniture.

Grønnegade 75 (tel: 62 61 06 45). Open: June to August, 10am–5pm daily; April, May, September and October, 10am–4pm daily; November to March 11am–3pm daily. Admission charge.

Gamle Gaard (Old Merchant's House)

This 1725 house contains a series of evocative tableaux recreating town life in the 18th and 19th centuries, the time when Fåborg was an important and prosperous trading post with one of the largest merchant fleets in Denmark. The sumptuous master bedroom, the kitchen and the beautifully planted garden featuring a summer pavilion, all demonstrate the enormous opulence which flowed in Fåborg during those centuries.

Holkegade 1 (tel: 62 61 33 38). Open: mid-May to mid-September 10.30am–4.30pm daily. Admission charge.

Fåborg is 37km south of Odense.

Old merchants' houses such as this, now a museum, recall Fåborg's glorious trading days

KERTEMINDE

Johannes Larsen, one of the foremost of the Funen Painters (see page 73), described this as 'the prettiest little town in the world, lying there deep in the bay by the mouth of the fjord'. Hyperbole, of course, but Kerteminde *is* the very epitome of a Danish fishing village with half-timbered houses, tarred huts, narrow cobbled alleys and a harbour abob with fishing boats. No matter that nowadays most of them take anglers out on day trips, and that the whole town has been sanitised for tourism. Larsen's birthplace has been converted into a bright, colourful little museum of local culture with a collection of his work.

Kerteminde is 22km east of Odense.

Larsen's Museum, Møllebakken (tel: 65 32 37 27). Open: 10am–4pm Tuesday to Sunday.

LANGELAND

Long spindly Langeland is one of the most popular islands in the Funen archipelago for sea and sand holidays; many families have summer houses here, and there are several camp sites. Although frequently windswept, the island's beaches are backed by sand dunes and speckled with marram grass where shelter can be taken if necessary. It is a prime location for windsurfing.

Away from the beaches and dunes, fertile Langeland is divided into neat fields of arable land and dairy pasture. At **Tranekær** a red fairytale castle rises out of the landscape (closed to the public, although the gardens and a windmill in the grounds can be visited). There is an excellent network of cycle tracks. The main town is **Rudkøbing** with its

Devotees of the Funen School make a pilgrimage to this house, Larsen's birthplace

Flat and green Langeland is a popular family resort

characterful old fishing port of half-timbered houses and cobbled lanes, as well as a modern yachting marina lined with open-air cafés. The **Langeland Museum** specialises in prehistoric and Viking finds from the island. **Det Gamle Apotek** (The Old Apothecary) has a collection of old pharmacists' paraphernalia.

Langeland, lying southeast of Fyn (Funen), is reached by road from Funen, via the island of Tåsinge, or by ferry and road from Fåborg via the island of Ærø.
Langeland Museum, Jens Winthersuej (tel: 62 51 13 47).
Open: May to September, closed Saturday.
Det Gamle Apotek, Brogade 15 (tel: 62 51 13 47). Open: June to August. Admission charge.

NYBORG

Over the last few years, Nyborg has been turned on its head by the presence of thousands of construction workers employed on the bridge and tunnel linking Funen with Zealand. Nyborg's strategic position, on the narrowest part of the Storebælt, was the reason why an indomitable castle was built here in the 12th century, around which the town grew up. The ancient castle, and the Storebælt project's **exhibition centre** (see page 68) represent the glorious juxtaposition of Denmark old and new.

Nyborg is 31km east of Odense.

Nyborg Slot (Nyborg Castle)

This was the greatest of a string of defensive castles built along the Storebælt in the 12th and 13th centuries. It became a royal palace, where various kings resided, until 1620 when storm damage was subsequently compounded by bombardment during the 1658–60 war with Sweden. Deemed no longer suitable for royalty, the castle fell into decay.

Restoration has been meticulous, with tours today capturing the medieval aura in the sparse, and echoing Great Hall, and the Danehof Hall, where the ancient parliament used to meet.

Slotsplasden, DK5800 Nyborg (tel: 65 31 02 07). Open: June to August, 10am–5pm daily; September to May, 10am–3pm Tuesday to Sunday. Admission charge.

Odense

*H*ans Christian Andersen (see page 80) welcomes visitors to the city of his birth in person. His pointed-nose profile flutters on thousands of bunting flags along the main shopping streets. He is to be seen in top hat and tail coat leading a troupe of fellow actors dressed as schoolchildren, in open-air productions of his fairytales. His ubiquity extends to statues, hotels and cafés bearing his name; books, cassettes and posters of and about him; and, of course, to the two museums dedicated to his life and works.

Before getting to grips with Andersenmania, it is worth remembering that Odense was an important city centuries before the great fairytale author was born. Its name means 'Odin's Shrine', referring to the Norse god of war. As the site of King Knud's murder, and later canonisation, the cathedral attracted Christian pilgrims throughout the Middle Ages. Later, with the building of a canal to Kerteminde on the Storebælt, Odense became an important commercial town. It remains Denmark's third largest city (after Copenhagen and Århus) and the administrative centre of Funen, despite an unhurried provincial atmosphere.

Several good museums testify to the richness of Odense's history, and most of the attractions are within easy walking distance of each other. With parks, open spaces and a river running through the town, Odense is airy, watery and relaxing, although the overall aspect is marred by a single, overbearing skyscraper. As a university town it is lively during term time, with many late-night cafés.

Odense tourist office, Rådhuset (tel: 66 12 75 20).

Brandts Klædefabrik (Brandt's Cloth Mill)

This former textile factory has been converted into an arts centre with a fast turnover of exhibitions in the bright and spacious shop floors once used for spinning and weaving. The emphasis in the main Kunsthallen (Art Gallery) is on up-and-coming international talent in the visual arts, sculpture, architecture, design and handicrafts. There is also the Museet for Fotokunst (Museum of Photographic Art), with a collection of classical photography as well as changing modern exhibitions; and the Danmarks Grafiske Museum (Danish Museum of Printing) charting the development of printing in Denmark over the past three centuries.

Brandts Passage 37 (tel: 66 12 10 20).
Open: 10am–5pm Monday to Friday,
11am–5pm weekends and holidays.
Admission charge.

Carl Nielsen Museet (Carl Nielsen Museum

Appropriately enough, this homage to
the life of Denmark's foremost composer
is located inside Odense's concert hall.

The museum traces Nielsen's life and
career through photographs, original
scores and extracts from both his early

and his later, more famous pieces,
played through headphones. There are
also selected examples from his writings,
such as *Springtime in Funen* and *My
Childhood* – memoirs from his early
years on the island. Nielsen's wife, Anne
Marie, was a well-known sculptress and
several of her works enliven the
museum.

Claus Bergs Gade 11 (tel: 66 13 13 72,
ext 4671). Open: 10am–4pm daily.
Admission charge.

ODENSE TOWN PLAN

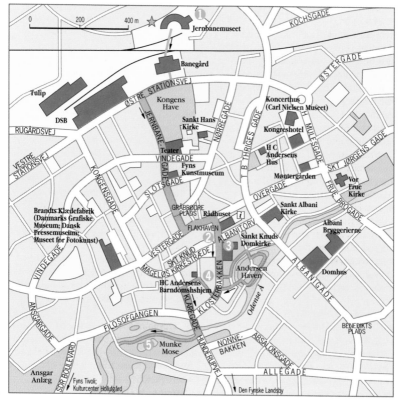

Pre-industrial life on show at Fynske Landsby

H C Andersens Hus (Hans Christian Andersen's House)

You've heard the fairy stories; now find out something about the man (see page 80). This is the main museum devoted to the writer's life, converted from several houses knocked together, including the one in which Andersen was born in 1805.

Since he was such a great hoarder of correspondence and personal effects, there is plenty for the serious Andersenologist to sift through – letters, photographs and original manuscripts of his work, which he wrote in several languages. Maps chart his many European travels, together with the voluminous trunks he took with him and a case containing his famous black top hat. A length of rope is also displayed – he is said to have taken it with him everywhere as a means of escape out of a fear of fire.

The circular central hall is splashed with murals illustrating Andersen's life, and, in a separate library, there is a huge collection of tomes of his work, in 70 different languages. There is also a collection of illustrations by Andersen himself, and by other artists inspired by his stories.

This museum should not be confused with the H C Andersen's Barndomshjem on Munkemøllestræde (see page 85), Andersen's home from the age of two, where there is a small exhibition illustrating his childhood.

Fynske Landsby (Funen Village)

A smithy, a cobbler's workshop, a village school, a watermill, a windmill, a merchant's house, workers' cottages, a prison house, a duck pond, farm animals and cobbled streets are just a few of the exhibits which make up this convincing display of life in a typical Funen village in the 18th and 19th centuries.

People in period costumes work at their crafts. Cattle-raising and agriculture are practised with the original methods. In other exhibitions, there are lifesized figures in authentic period costumes. Many of the tools, artefacts and ornaments are genuine period pieces. If they were to spread more manure about, instead of keeping the village spotlessly clean, the transport back in time would be complete.

Sejerskovvej 20 (tel: 66 13 13 72). Open: June to August, 10am–5.30pm daily; April to May and September to mid-October, 10am–4pm Sundays and holidays; mid-October to March, exhibitions closed but free entrance to the park. Admission charge. Bus 21 or 22 from Odense centre.

Hans Jensens Stræde 37–45 (tel: 66 13 13 72, ext 4665). Open: January to May and September to December, 10am–4pm daily; June to August, 9am–6pm daily. Admission charge.

Møntergården (Museum of Cultural and Urban History)

This museum in a run of adjoining 16th- and 17th-century half-timbered houses, is far less dry than its name suggests. Odense's pre-Andersen era is brought imaginatively to life through a chronological series of life-sized tableaux, backed up by archaeological finds such as coins, medals and tools. The town's history is covered, from the Vikings, through medieval craftsmen, to the work of the Dominican friars.

Overgade 48–50 (tel: 66 13 13 72). Open: 10am–4pm daily. Admission charge.

Sankt Knuds Domkirke (Saint Canute's Cathedral)

This is one of Denmark's major cathedrals, a vast Gothic structure built in the 13th century. Its bright, airy, whitewashed and frescoed interior hides some architectural and spiritual treasures which are often ignored in a city more focused on fairytales and modern art.

Be sure not to miss the magnificent gold and wood-carved altarpiece, or the worn steps down to the tombs of Saint Canute and Saint Alban. (Some experts believe that the latter may actually be the remains of Canute's brother, Benedict.) Time and quiet are needed here.

Sankt Knud Kirkestræde. Open: 10am–4pm Monday to Saturday. Admission free.

Murals in Andersen's house recall stories from the writer's life

HANS CHRISTIAN ANDERSE

Once upon a time the washerwoman wife of a poor cobbler gave birth to a son in a tumbledown cottage at Odense, on the Danish island of Funen. The year was 1805 and the infant, Hans Christian Andersen, grew up to become the most famous Dane who has ever lived. His fairytales and other writings have been translated into more than 100 languages.

From an early age young Andersen's talents shone through, though never focused on any single discipline; he painted, sang, danced and acted. His father died when he was 11

and he was left in the care of his paternal grandmother. Three years later he set off for Copenhagen to seek his fortune, dreaming of fame as an actor or ballet dancer.

But Andersen's life was dogged by disappointment and sadness, all of which is recorded in his personal diaries and his autobiography *The Story of My Life* (1847). Although he attended the Royal Theatre School, he never achieved more than a walk-on part as a troll. It was made clear to him that his ambitions on the ballet stage would be thwarted by his physical appearance – his nose was large and he was generally considered ugly. He felt lonely and unloved, suffering particularly from an unrequited passion for the Swedish singer, Jenny Lind.

And yet, it was his unhappiness and loneliness that gave rise to his extraordinary creativity as a writer of fairy stories. The poignancy of *The Ugly Duckling*, for example, comes straight from the heart. The Chinese Emperor's yearning for *The Nightingale* is his own for Jenny Lind (whose nickname was 'the Swedish Nightingale'). Even so, his fairy stories all end happily, reflecting the fact that sadness never embittered him. Without

his essential warmth and humanity,
these and other immortal classics, such
as *The Princess and the Pea*, and *The
Little Mermaid,* could not have touched
the hearts and minds of countless
millions of children and adults.

The fame and fortune he achieved
appears not to have fulfilled him, nor
did it assuage his sadness or still his
restlessness. He mixed with the rich
and famous, but always lived in
temporary accommodation, never
putting down roots. He was a
passionate traveller who toured Europe
29 times before his death in 1875.

Andersen's immortal fairy story characters
are known all over the globe

Above: the market place at Svendborg
Left: a sign in Ærøskobing, on Ærø

SVENDBORG

Svendborg is Funen's second largest city, and the gateway to Tåsinge, Langeland, Ærø (see page 70) and the Funen archipelago's smaller southern islands. The upper town has commanding views out over the islands and along the south Funen coast. Steep, narrow and winding streets lead down to the sheltered harbour, which was once the Hanseatic trading port on which Svendborg's prosperity was built and is now a major yachting marina. It is also the start and finishing point of the Fyn Rundt wooden ships race, held each July.

Svendborgsund bridge spans more than 1km of water across to Tåsinge.

Svendborg is 24km east of Fåborg.

TÅSINGE

Although for many people Tåsinge island is no more than a staging post on the way from Funen to Langeland, a stop here has its rewards. Those who turn off the main road at the end of the bridge from Svendborg find that the atmosphere changes suddenly to one of gentle seclusion. This is a very green and gently undulating agricultural island, sprinkled with orchards, ponds and thatched farmhouses. Its gem is the immaculately preserved little village of **Troense**, with half-timbered waterfront houses looking over a yacht harbour and across the narrow stretch of water to tiny Thurø. Valdemars Castle is just outside the village.

Tåsinge lies south of Funen, 1km south of the port of Svendborg.

Valdemars Slot (Valdemar's Castle)

Like many Danish castles, this is really more of a stately mansion. It was built by Christian IV between 1639 and 1644 for his son, Count Valdemar Christian (hence the name), who died in battle soon afterwards. Its princely character was enhanced by naval hero Niels Juel, in 1678, who was presented with the castle as a reward for his exploits in the wars against Sweden. He added the sumptuous baroque-style royal apartment and halls. The vast kitchen and candle-lit chapel are also worth seeing.

When the museum is closed, the grounds are still worth visiting; wander up from the sandy beach just moments away, and gaze at the imposing façade across an ornamental lake.

Valdemars Slot Herregårdsmuseum, Slotsallén 100, 1km east of Troense (tel: 62 22 61 06). Open: from Easter, 10am–5pm Saturday, Sunday and holidays; May to September, 10am–5pm daily; October, 10am–5pm Saturday, Sunday and school holidays. Admission charge.

Valdemar's Castle, dating from the 17th century

Odense

This gentle amble takes in the pedestrianised heart of Odense, passing through gardens and along the river, to give you a feel for a city that reflects the peace and gentleness of the island whose capital it is. For map, see page 77.
Allow 2 hours.

The walk starts outside the railway station where the Railway Museum is worth exploring.

1 JERNBANEMUSEET (RAILWAY MUSEUM)

The museum covers the history of Danish railways, illustrated by real and model locomotives and carriages dating back 150 years.

Modern sculptures of ancient playthings at Odense, world capital of the fairytale

Leave the museum via the railway station and follow Jernbanegade southwards, passing the Fyns Kunstmuseum (Funen Art Gallery) on the left at No 13 (tel: 66 13 13 72, ext 4652; open: 10am–4pm daily, plus 7–10pm Wednesday). Turn left at the end of the road, following Vestergade into Flakhaven.

2 FLAKHAVEN

Flakhaven marks the heart of the historic red-brick city centre. The statue of Frederik VII is juxtaposed with a rather bizarre abstract sculpture. Dominating the square is the imperious 57m-long façade of the 1883 **Rådhuset**, in a jumble of architectural styles. The interior can be visited to see a variety of paintings by Funen artists, including Johannes Larsen. The tourist office is also inside.
Cross to the south of the square and enter the cathedral (see page 79) which is frequently empty of visitors, despite being one of the finest in Denmark.

Hans Christian Andersen and his characters parade along the Odense riverbank

3 SANKT KNUDS DOMKIRKE (SAINT CANUTE'S CATHEDRAL)

One of the cathedral's secret treats is to creep into the crypt, following in the footsteps of millions of earlier pilgrims whose feet have worn down the stone stairs that lead to the tombs of Saints Canute and Alban (Sankt Albani).

Follow a path from the cathedral down to the grassy bank of the Odense Å (Odense river) and cross a wooden footbridge on to the H C Andersen Haven (gardens) on an island. Note the metal sculptures of Andersen's fairytale characters which appear to be floating on the calm lake. Follow the path round the island and leave it via the third footbridge leading into Klosterbakken. Take the first turning on the right for Munkemøllestræde. The tiny house at Nos 3–5 is where Andersen lived from the age of two until his departure for Copenhagen at 14.

4 H C ANDERSENS BARNDOMSHJEM (HOUSE)

The author described this house as having 'One single room where all the space was taken up by the workshop, the bed and the bench where I slept'. The house in fact has two rooms; the other was occupied by another family.

Leaving the house, retrace your footsteps a few paces and turn right, cutting through to Klaregade, which leads over the river. Turn immediately right on to a footpath through the gardens.

5 MUNKEMOSE (GARDENS)

Finish the walk by wandering through this expanse of greenery and herbaceous borders, looking across the River Odense with its overhanging willows, anglers and flotillas of ducks.

> **Railway Museum**, 24 Dannebrogsgade (tel: 66 12 01 48). Open: May to September daily, 10am–4pm; October to April Tuesday to Sunday, 10am–1pm. Admission charge.
>
> **Rådhuset**, Flakhaven (tel: 66 13 13 72). Open: 9am–3.30pm Monday to Wednesday, 9am–5.30pm Thursday, 9am–noon Friday. Admission charge.
>
> **H C Anderson's House** (tel: 66 13 13 72 ext 4665). Open: June to September 10am–5pm daily; October to May 11am–3pm. Admisssion charge.

South Funen by Bike

This ride passes through some of Funen's most enchanting landscapes, exploring small villages, hidden lanes and historic houses. The steeper gradients require some effort, and there are plentiful opportunities for short walking detours. *Allow 3 hours.*

Starting in Fåborg, hire a bicycle from Bjarnes Cykler on Svendborgvej 69 and set off eastwards along the waterfront road, turning left on to the signposted cycle Route 51 (Road No 44). After about 2km of gentle uphill cycling, a mill comes into view on the right.

1 KALEKO MØLLE

This is the oldest working watermill in Denmark, parts of it dating to the 17th century. Inside is a small museum arranged with old furniture and objects illustrating the home and working

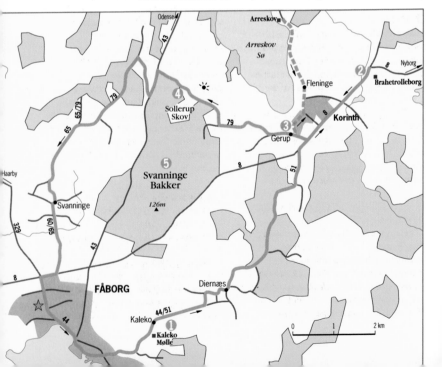

life of a miller and his family in the 19th century. Next to the mill is the stream and millpond, an old barn and a stable all set amid fields and with woodland beyond. *Continue up Route 51, through Korinth. On the right-hand side of the straight road just beyond the village look for a large manor house with a church and spire alongside.*

2 BRAHETROLLEBORG

Originally a Cistercian monastery from 1172, parts of this large manor-house complex, including the church and outbuildings, date from the 13th century. Further remains of the monastery were discovered during restoration work in 1985. The park is open to the public. *Return the short distance to Korinth and turn right (westwards) on to Cycle Route 79 – a leafy lane that meanders into the hills. After about 1km, you reach Gerup.*

3 GERUP

The old school building, built in 1784, is one of the oldest in Denmark. It has been turned into a small school museum illustrating the changing life of teachers and pupils at rural schools from the 18th to the 20th centuries.

From here, if you have time, it is worth turning right to detour beside the narrow lake as far as Arreskov manor house on the left, before returning to Route 79. *Continue for about another 2km to the Sollerup viewpoint and picnic spot on the right.*

4 SOLLERUP SKOV (SOLLERUP WOODS)

There are beautiful views over Arreskov Sø, Funen's largest lake, and the undulating hills and forest beyond. *Continue along Cycle Route 79, bearing left at its junction with Cycle Route 65 (Road No 43) turning south. Soon the high spire of Svanninge's church comes into view.*

5 SVANNINGE BAKKER (NATURE PARK)

In typically Danish self-deprecating fashion, these gentle, wooded hills of winding lanes and country houses, are often called the 'Funen Alps'. At the farm 'Kastanjely', in Svanninge village, information is available on footpaths and nature trails in the Svanninge Bakker (Nature Park), together with explanations of the flora, fauna and geology. The highest point is 126m above sea level. At the top of one 85m hill is a tower that can be climbed, free of charge, for a 360-degree panorama. *From Svanninge continue gently downhill on Cycle Route 60, then Cycle Route 65 to Road No 8. Turn right, then immediately left on to Road No 44 which will take you back to Fåborg.*

> **Kaleko Mølle**, Prices Havevej, Diernæs (tel: 62 61 33 38). Open: mid-May to mid-September, 10.30am–4.30pm daily. Admission charge.
> **Brahetrolleborg**, Reventlowsvej 1, Korinth, Fåborg (tel: 61 65 10 04). Open: mid-April to mid-October daily, 8am–4pm. Admission charge.

Jutland (Jylland)

*J*utland is Denmark's 'finger', the northwards-pointing peninsula that accounts for around 70 per cent of the country's land area, though only about 45 per cent of its population. Since Viking times, Denmark's power has been focused eastwards on Zealand, leaving Jutland characterised by its calm people and peaceful countryside. Like the rest of the peninsula, the main cities of Århus and Aalborg (which are the nation's second and fourth largest respectively in terms of population) are distinctly provincial in feeling when compared with cosmopolitan Copenhagen.

Between the German border and the tip of Jutland (about 400km to the north) the peninsula divides into three distinct geographical areas, each differing markedly in scenery and atmosphere. **South Jutland** is flat and marshy, with

large herds of cattle grazing fertile pastures. Modern aerogenerators contrast strikingly with ancient market towns, such as Ribe and Tønder. The region's history is entwined with that of its neighbour, Germany. Southern Jutland, then called North Sleswig, was captured by Prussia in 1864, and returned to Denmark in 1920 after a plebiscite.

Denmark at its gentlest is found in **Mid-Jutland**. The countryside of the so-called 'Lake District' is rippled with hills and sprinkled with lakes, forests and streams; on the east coast, villages huddle round safe harbours. Everything appears to be on a miniature scale, as if a parody of Danish understatement.

The Limfjord slices right through Jutland, from the North Sea to the Baltic. Beyond the fjord, the scenery of **North Jutland** becomes more rugged; the cosy atmosphere is discarded for something wilder, more exposed and closer to nature in the raw. There are superb beaches, great bald sand dunes and splintering inlets, redolent of Norway. At Skagen, on the peninsula's northern extremity, there is a sense of continuous climax as the two seas meet.

North Sea ferries land at Esbjerg, also Scandinavia's largest fishing port

JUTLAND

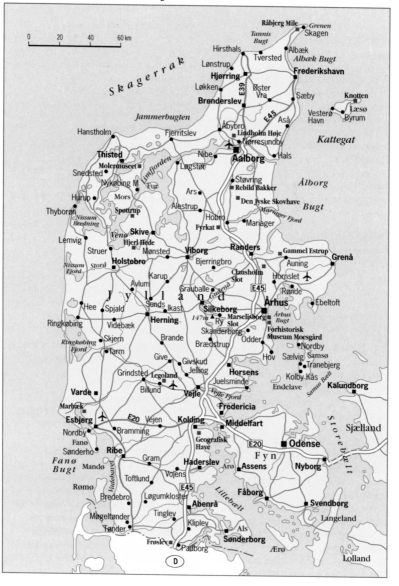

AALBORG TOWN PLAN

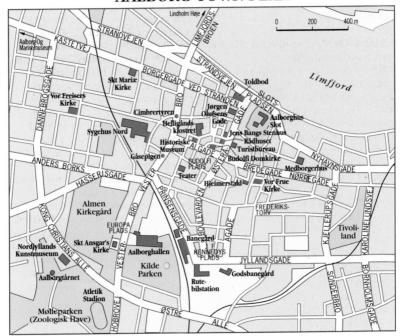

AALBORG

Throughout Scandinavia the name of Denmark's fourth largest city is linked to Aquavit, the highly popular grain spirit, flavoured with caraway seeds, that is distilled here. Natives of the city, however, appear to be more intoxicated on their rich history and heritage. Their pride in all things traditional is reflected in the fact that when, in 1948, the Danish double A was changed to Å (as in Århus, for example), the city refused to comply. So Aalborg it is, although the sacrilegious Ålborg is sometimes used.

Aalborg was founded in Viking times, at the narrowest point on the Limfjord, its strategic location making it an important transport junction for trade with Norway and Sweden. Today the city remains an important industrial centre.

Aalborg is 109km north of Århus. Aalborg tourist office is at Østerågade 8 (tel: 98 12 60 22).

Aalborg Historiske Museum (Historical Museum)

This museum is well worth visiting for the 1602 Aalborg Room – a chamber of wood-carved panelling and coffered ceilings all taken from a wealthy merchant's house and painstakingly reassembled. Other displays span the city's history from the Stone Age through to the present.

Algade 48 (tel: 98 12 45 22). Open: 10am–5pm Tuesday to Saturday. Admission charge.

Aalborg-Og Marinemuseum (Marine and Naval Museum)

Climb aboard the *Springeren*, a real submarine over 50m long, and wander its claustrophobic corridors and conning tower. There are several other retired naval vessels in this shipyard on the Limfjord, as well as an excellent oceanography section where you can measure the current and water temperature in the fjord.

Vestre Fjordvej 81 (tel: 98 11 78 03). Open: March to December. Admission charge.

Budolfi Domkirke (St Botolph's Cathedral)

The carillon that plays every hour (from 9am to 10pm) will tell in which direction to head. Most of the whitewashed brick church was built around 1400, although some remnants survive of a church 300 years older. The baroque spire was added in 1779. Inside, the vast altarpiece, the marble font and the fine carved pulpit are worth a look, but the real treasures of this cathedral are the superb frescos. The entrance porch is itself a former chapel adorned with pictorial representations of Abraham's sacrifice of Isaac, and the touching legend of the fig tree that bowed down to the infant Jesus on the flight to Egypt. On the south wall are some wonderfully colourful frescos of centaurs and the life of St Catherine of Alexandria.

Algade. Open: 10am–4pm Monday to Friday and 10am–noon Saturday. Admission free.

Jens Bang's Stenhus (Jens Bang's House)

This grand five-storey mansion of 1624 is the largest Renaissance building in Scandinavia. Bang was a wealthy merchant who surrounded himself with splendour, but it is the eccentricities reflecting his personality that attract most attention.

Argumentative and obstinate, he made many enemies and caricatured them in the shape of the grotesque gargoyles that can been seen on the façade. The face looking out on the south side, rudely sticking its tongue out at the Rådhuset, is said to represent Bang himself expressing his disgust at his failure to be elected to the town council.

The building is still a pharmacy, as it has been for over 300 years. The vaulted basement was a secret meeting place for the Danish Resistance during the war, and is now a very popular and atmospheric wine bar.

Østerågade 9, next to the tourist office.

St Botolph's, a 15th-century cathedral at the heart of a modern city

Lindholm Høje: there was no greater honour for a Viking warrior than to die in battle

Nordjyllands Kunstmuseum (North Jutland Arts Museum)

The white marble and glass exterior of this ultra-modern building, located at the edge of an expansive wooded park, sets the scene. Inside is one of the most important collections of modern art in Denmark. Natural light streams into the galleries where the exhibits can be viewed in their extravagant, wide open display areas. Contemporary Danish artists predominate, but there are also works by Andy Warhol and Max Ernst. Youngsters can discard any inhibitions in the children's section, where they can touch exhibits and make as much noise as they want.

Outside, the sculpture park is dominated by Bjørn Nørgaard's acclaimed **Dream Palace**, a pyramid made of glass. There is also an amphitheatre where open-air plays and concerts are held in summer.

Kong Christians Allé 50 (tel: 98 13 80 88). Open: July and August, 10am–5pm daily; September to June, 10am–5pm Tuesday to Sunday. Admission charge.

Nearby
LINDHOLM HØJE

This Iron Age and Viking settlement and burial ground is one of the most important archaeological sites in Denmark. Nearly 700 graves have been excavated and the finds are displayed in the museum to the west of the site. The museum also has a series of tableaux illustrating life and social structures in the village.

The remains of this were found, perfectly preserved, in 1952, having been buried by drifting sand in about AD1000.

Lindholm Høje is at Nørresundby, which lies north of the Limfjord, directly opposite Aalborg to which it is connected by a bridge and tunnel. From Aalborg take bus No 6 (Uttrup Nord).

Vendilavej 11, 9400 Nørresundby (tel: 98 17 55 22). Open: June to August, 10am–7pm daily; September to mid-October, 10am–5pm daily; mid-October to Easter, 10am–4pm Tuesday to Sunday; Easter to 31 May, 10am–5pm daily. Admission charge.

ÅRHUS see pages 114–17.

BILLUND

The village of Billund is overshadowed by **Legoland** (see page 106) and by the international airport, built there because of its commercially strategic position right in the geographical centre of Jutland. Less publicised, but also worth seeing, is the **Billund Center Mobilium** which, like Legoland, is within walking distance of the airport terminal. Three museums are under one roof: the **Danmarks Flyvemuseum** (Aviation Museum), including some early flying machines, the **Danmarks Bilmuseum (Car Museum)**, with more than 70 vintage

cars and motorcycles, and the **Falck Museet**, dedicated to the history of the fire and ambulance services.

Billund is 60km southwest of Århus. Ellehammers Alle 3 (tel: 75 35 32 22). Open: June to mid-September, 10am–7pm daily; mid-September to May, 10am–4pm Saturday and Sunday. Admission charge.

CLAUSHOLM SLOT (CLAUSHOLM CASTLE)

More a mansion than a castle, this is one of the finest pieces of baroque architecture in Denmark. Built at the end of the 17th century for the Lord

Clausholm Castle features some of the finest baroque architecture in the country

Chancellor, Count Conrad Rewentlow, it became the home of his daughter, Queen Anna Sophie, after the death of King Frederik IV. There are beautiful stucco ceilings, Denmark's oldest organ (in the chapel) and some fine formal gardens.

Clausholm Slot is 31km north of Århus. Clausholhvej 308, Voldum (tel: 86 49 16 01). Open: mid-June to mid-August. Admission charge.

CASTLES, MANORS AND

Castles, manor houses and beautiful churches are an inescapable part of any visit to Denmark. They are also a key to understanding this tiny nation's extraordinary past.

Centuries of warfare left Denmark's strategic points defended by sturdy medieval fortresses. Yet Denmark's grandest castles date from the Renaissance period, as the austere styles born of defensive needs gradually gave way to the architectural influences seeping across Europe. **Kronenborg Castle** at Helsingør (see page 52) is a glorious example of 17th-century Renaissance splendour set within huge medieval ramparts that look threateningly across the Øresund to Sweden. **Egeskov Castle** on Funen (see page 72) is a purer example of

Renaissance architecture, with its moat and turrets retained for aesthetic, rather than defensive, purposes.

The manor houses that punctuate the Danish countryside are also fruits of peaceful times, when a wealthy, land-owning class felt safe enough to build themselves fine residences. Very few gave way to ostentation, however; they tend rather to reflect the understated beauty and modest scale of Denmark. Many of these fine homes have now

Right: Renaissance Egeskov Castle
Below: Kronenborg Castle at Helsingør, where Hamlet pondered life's ultimate question

CHURCHES

Colourful frescos on white backgrounds give Danish churches a light, airy feeling

been converted to museums or country house hotels.

The churches and cathedrals at the heart of most Danish towns are refreshingly airy compared to the dark interiors of many European churches. Whitewashed interiors, frescoed walls and brilliantly gilded altarpieces seem to radiate joy in small town churches, while towering wonders, such as **Roskilde Cathedral** with its royal tombs (see page 56), speak of the powerful role of the Church in Danish history.

Søndersø, one of Funen's simpler churches

EBELTOFT

This idyllic holiday town has a long cobbled main street, lined with half-timbered houses, running parallel to the harbour. At its heart is **Det Gamle Rådhuset** (the Old Town Hall), claimed as the world's smallest, housing the Ebeltoft Museum with changing exhibitions about the town and its environs.

Ebeltoft's most popular attraction, however, is the recently overhauled triple-masted *Jylland* frigate – the world's longest wooden ship. Active in the Danish Navy (from its launch in 1860 until 1887), a veteran of the battle of Heligoland and a former royal yacht, the *Jylland* has been completely restored to its original condition, making a glorious sight, moored on the Strandvej quayside. A short way along the Strandvej is the **Glasmuseum** (Glass Museum), housing Denmark's largest exhibition of modern glass.

Ebeltoft is 54km east of Århus. The Ebeltoft/Mols tourist office is at Strandvejen 2 (tel: 86 34 14 00).

Ebeltoft Museum, Torvet (tel: 86 34 13 82). Open: April and May, 1–4pm Tuesday to Friday; June to August, 10am–5pm Tuesday to Sunday; October to March, 1–4pm Tuesday to Friday and 1–6pm Saturday and Sunday. Admission charge.

Fregatten Jylland, Strandvejen 6 (tel: 86 34 10 99). Open: June to August, 10am–9pm daily; September, October, March and April, 10am–5pm daily; November to March, 10am–4pm daily. Admission charge.

Glasmuseum, Strandvejen 8 (tel: 86 34 17 99). Open: October to April, 1–4pm Monday to Saturday and 10am–4pm Sunday; May, June and September, 10am–5pm daily; July, 10am–9pm daily. Admission charge.

ESBJERG

Esbjerg is the port of disembarkation for visitors arriving in Denmark by ferry from across the North Sea. Few other tourists choose to visit the mainly modern, industrial port, which is Denmark's fifth largest city. It is also the largest fishing port in Scandinavia, with a vast fish-processing factory, as you can tell from the odour that frequently hangs over the town.

Esbjerg is on Jutland's west coast, 90km southwest of Århus. The tourist office is at Skolegade 33, Torvet (tel: 75 12 55 99).

Fiskeriog Søfartmuseet (Fisheries and Maritime Museum)

The sight not to miss is this museum just north of the town, where the history of commercial

The gleaming ship's bell of the wooden frigate *Jylland*

Seals perform their aquabatics at Esbjerg's Fisheries and Maritime Museum

fishing and the changing life of fishermen is imaginatively displayed in a series of exhibits. There are several reconditioned and refitted fishing boats from different eras that can be entered and explored, and some rebuilt fishermen's houses.

The museum also has an aquarium and sealarium. Instead of the selection of exotic specimens common to most aquariums, this one is largely devoted to the Atlantic and Baltic fish on which the industry depends. The seals can be watched underwater through the glass wall of their tank. There is great excitement for children at feeding time.

Saltvandsakvariet, Tarphagevej (tel: 75 15 06 66). Open: mid-May to 30 June and September, 10am–6pm daily; July and August,10am–8pm daily; October to mid-May,10am–4pm daily. Feeding time is at 10am and 2.30pm. Admission charge.

Esbjerg Museum
The city's main museum has two separate exhibitions, both worth a quick visit. The first demonstrates life in the city between 1890 and 1940 with some authentic tableaux, and explains how the fishing and mercantile port burgeoned into a major city. The second, more recent, exhibition is of earlier life in the area and on nearby Fanø (see page 98). A small museum of amber is also housed here.

Torvegade 45 (tel: 75 12 78 11). Open: June to October; 10am–4pm daily. Closed: Mondays from September to May. Admission charge.

Frederikshavn feels as much Norwegian and Swedish as Danish

FANØ

Just 20 minutes by ferry across a narrow strip of water from Esbjerg, Fanø is the city's playground. The island is 18km long with a forested interior criss-crossed by footpaths and cycling trails. In summer the main attraction is the long sandy beach on the west coast, where many families have holiday homes. There are also several camp sites.

The main village is **Nordby** where there are two good museums. The **Fanø Museum** charts the evolving lifestyle of the Fanø islanders and has a collection of oddities from around the world brought back by sailors. The **Fanø Søfarts-og Dragtudstilling Museum** (Maritime and Costume Museum) displays model ships and local dress from throughout the ages. Quaint little thatched and half-timbered houses make **Sønderho** village, to the south, worth visiting.

Fanø Museum (tel: 75 16 26 00). Open: June and October, 10am–1pm; July, 10am–noon and 2–5pm.

Maritime and Costume Museum (tel: 75 16 22 72). Open: May to September, Monday to Saturday 10am–5pm.
The Fanø tourist office is at Havnepladsen, Nordby (tel: 75 16 26 00).

The Fanø ferry (tel: 33 14 88 80) takes 20 minutes, leaving from Esbjerg harbour every half hour from May to September and every hour from October to April.

FJERRITSLEV

Fjerritslev is the principal tourist town of Han Herred – the land between the Limfjorden and the sea. With several hotels and a scattering of holiday homes, it makes an excellent base for exploring the beaches and countryside of North Jutland. The town is also home to the **Fjerritslev Bryggeri-og Egnsmuseum** (Fjerritslev Brewing Museum) next to the tourist office. The museum is housed in the Kjeldgaard brewery which closed in 1968 but has been preserved intact with gleamingly polished brass.

Immediately north of Fjerritslev there

is more than 30km of fine sandy beach. From Road No 11, tracks lead through the dunes to the popular swimming areas of **Tranum Strand**, **Torup Strand** and **Bulbjerg**.

Fjerritslev is 120km northwest of Århus, and 40km west of Aalborg.
Fjerritslev Brewing Museum open: June to September, 10am–4.30pm Monday to Friday.
The tourist office is at Østergade 1 (tel: 08 21 16 55).

FREDERIKSHAVN
Frederikshavn is one of North Jutland's main ports, with ferry connections to various Norwegian and Swedish cities (including Oslo and Gothenburg) and to the remote island of Læso (see page 140). Around the fishing harbour is a small district of narrow streets and cottages, mostly painted yellow. There is also a much larger shopping district, of pedestrianised precincts, where hordes of visitors from around Scandinavia come to shop for bargains in food, clothes and drink. Just outside the town is the **Bangsbo** manor house and deer park.

Frederikshavn is 60km northeast of Aalborg. The tourist office is at Brotorvet 1 (tel: 98 42 32 66).

FRØSLEV
In 1944 the occupying Germans established a concentration camp at Frøslev, where some 13,000 Danes were held. Although the sort of atrocities perpetrated by the Nazis elsewhere did not happen here, some Danes suffered greatly when they were deported to other concentration camps in Germany. After the war, Danish collaborators were held here awaiting trial.

Some of the blocks at Frøslev have been preserved with their tight-packed bunk accommodation. The original main watchtower stands intimidatingly above. Other blocks house three small museums (with separate entrance charges). One illustrates the work of the Danish Red Cross Organisation from World War II until the present; the second demonstrates the work of Danish troops serving with the United Nations, including a force currently in Bosnia; the third, an exhibition mounted by Amnesty International, illustrates the extent of human-rights violations around the world.

Frøslev is on the Danish/German frontier, 60km south of Kolding. Museet for Froeslevlejren, Lejrvejen 83, Padborg (tel: 74 67 65 57). Open: April to October, 10am–5pm daily. Admission charge.

A simple and moving memorial to the wartime dead at Frøslev's former German concentration camp, which now includes three museums

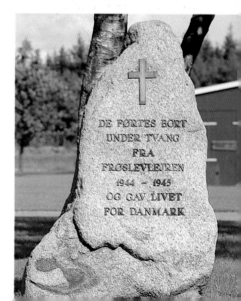

Like most aristocratic homes in Denmark, Gammel Estrup houses a museum

GAMMEL ESTRUP

The 16th-century Renaissance moated manor house castle of Gammel Estrup was the home for generations of two noble families – first the Broks and latterly the Scheels – both close advisors to the Crown. After the death of Count Scheel (in 1936) his heirs sold the castle and contents, but two years later it was bought by his son-in-law, Valdemar Uttental, and the **Jyllands Herregårdsmuseum** (Jutland Manor House Museum) was established here. Many of the original furnishings and works of art have been re-acquired and are displayed in a sequence of styles, changing from room to room, following the character of each generation to live in the castle.

The **Dansk Landbrugsmuseum** (Danish Agricultural Museum) is housed in a separate building within the castle grounds. Thousands of agricultural implements are displayed, with exhibitions explaining the evolution of farming over the last two centuries. Changing exhibitions of agriculturally themed paintings, sculpture, ceramics and textiles are also staged.

Gammel Estrup is in the village of Auning, 38km north of Århus.

Jyllands Herregårdsmuseum (tel: 86 48 30 01). Open: April to September, 10am–5pm daily; October to March, 11am–3pm Tuesday to Sunday. Admission charge. Dansk Landbrugsmuseum (tel: 86 48 34 44). Open: 10am–5pm daily. Admission charge.

HOBRO

Strategically positioned at the head of the Mariager Fjord (see page 108), Hobro was founded as a Viking settlement in AD980 and is a good base for exploring the region. Many archaeological finds from Fyrkat (see below) are housed in the **Hobro Museum**, as well as collections of glass, porcelain and silver.

Hobro is 46km south of Aalborg. The tourist office is at Store Torv (tel: 98 52 56 66).

Hobro Museum, Vestergade 21–23 (tel: 98 57 05 55). Open: April to October, 11am–5pm daily . Admission charge.

Nearby
Fyrkat, 3km west of Hobro, is one of only four known Viking forts in Denmark. It is believed to have been built as a military base, on the orders of Harald Bluetooth, in around AD980. The smallest of the four, Fyrkat was constructed of wooden staves with a precision and strict symmetry rare anywhere in the Viking world. It has been rebuilt with equal attention to detail, with circular ramparts enclosing three rooms where once around 50 people lived.

A reproduction Viking house outside the fort, and a Viking farm about 500m away, demonstrate life in the 10th century, based on knowledge gained from excavating the site.

Vikingecenter Fyrkat, Fyrkatvej 37D og 45 (tel: 98 51 09 27). Open: 10am–5pm daily. Admission charge.

HOLSTEBRO
Five major roads converge at this market town on the River Storå, which staged one of Denmark's greatest medieval ox fairs. A series of major fires destroyed the historic heart of the town, although the 1907 church does contain several

treasures from its incinerated predecessor, including a superb 16th-century Dutch altarpiece and a 48-bell carillon.

Holstebro has compensated for its loss with two excellent art galleries. The **Holstebro Art Museum** exhibits a large and varied collection of contemporary Danish work, plus ethnic art from Bali, Peru, Tibet and various parts of Africa. The **Jens Nielsen and Olivia Holm-Møller Collection** is composed largely of the works of these two artists, supplemented with works by other Danish artists.

Holstebro is 52km west of Viborg. The tourist office is at Brotorvet 8 (tel: 97 42 57 00).

Holstebro Kunstmuseum, Hernongvej 1 (tel: 97 42 45 18). Open: noon–4pm Tuesday to Sunday. Admission charge.

Jens Nielsen and Olivia Holm-Møller Collection, Nørrebrogade 1 (tel: 97 42 18 24). Open: noon–4pm Tuesday to Sunday. Admission charge.

Archaeological work at Fyrkat has provided vital insights into Viking life

FARMING

Some visitors to Denmark expect to encounter vast herds of swine snuffling and grunting their way through the countryside. So renowned has Danish bacon become, that along with pastries and blue cheese, the country and product are automatically associated in millions of minds across Europe and further afield.

In fact, you could easily drive from one end of Denmark to the other without ever glimpsing a pink snout or curly tail. Nor, in a score of lavish breakfast buffets, would you necessarily so much as sniff at a rasher of streaky bacon. Danish pigs are intensively farmed, often indoors, and the canny Danes export almost all of the meat. Not only does Danish bacon grace millions of British, Dutch and German breakfast tables, huge quantities of fresh pork constitute Denmark's single most lucrative export to Japan. On the basis of this, Denmark is the only European Union country to enjoy a trade surplus with Japan.

In truth, the ultra-efficient farming of pigs is only one facet of the sweeping revolution which has calmly taken place under the gentle, placid exterior of the Danish countryside. In 1960 there were around 200,000 farms employing 20 per cent of the population. Today, there are nearly 80,000 farms with agriculture employing just 6 per cent of the population. The average size of a farm

Bucolic scenes in the Danish countryside, but much of the farming is, in fact, intensive

is around 35ha, with most holdings being worked almost exclusively by the families that own them. Half the country's agricultural land is under cereals, and 20 per cent is used as grazing pasture; most of the remainder is used either for rearing pigs and other livestock, or for growing beet.

The success of Danish farming can be attributed to the efficient co-operative societies set up to market and distribute Danish farm produce.

The other ingredient is the strict rationalisation of farming that has led Denmark to produce a limited range of produce, but to do so extremely well.

HORSENS

This commercial and industrial town, at the head of the broad Horsens Fjord, dates from the 12th century. First impressions, however, are of a more modern town, especially along Søndergade, the wide pedestrianised main shopping street. There you will find the grand façade of the **Jørgensen Hotel**, the former Lichtenberg Palace, built for a rich merchant in1744. For a more intimate sense of Horsens, turn down any of the narrow traffic-free side streets leading off the Søndergade. The main square in the town centre is dedicated to Horsens' most famous son, the explorer and cartographer Vitus Bering (1680–1741), after whom the Bering Sea and Straits are named.

The small town has several museums, and the one not to be missed is the **Industrimuseet** (Museum of Industry), which has some wonderful old industrial machinery gleamingly restored.

A tower is required to lend 'Sky Mountain', Denmark's highest point, a hint of credibility

Horsens is 40km southwest of Århus. The tourist office is at Søndergade 26 (tel: 75 62 38 22).

Industrimuseet, Gasvej 17–19 (tel: 75 62 07 88). Open: July and August, 10am–4pm daily; September to June, 11am–4pm Tuesday to Sunday. Admission charge.

KOLDING

Founded in the 13th century, Kolding is one of the most important junction towns in East Jutland, with roads converging upon it from all parts of the peninsula. The town is dominated by the massive **Koldinghus Castle**, originally built by King Erik V in 1268 but almost entirely rebuilt by various later monarchs. The earliest preserved sections are 15th century. In the 18th century it fell into disrepair. A lengthy period of rebuilding started in 1890, to create the museum which today contains an awesome collection of Romanesque and Gothic church sculpture, furniture, early Danish painting, ceramics and silver. From the top of the Giants' Tower there are superb views over the town.

Kolding is 70km southwest of Århus. The tourist office is at Akseltorv 8 (tel: 75 53 21 00).

Museet på Koldinghus (tel: 75 50 15 00; weekends 75 50 16 52). Open: April to September, 10am–5pm daily; October to March, noon–3pm Monday to Friday and 10am–3pm Saturday, Sunday and public holidays. Admission charge.

LAKE DISTRICT

In many ways, Denmark's Lake District reflects the character of the country as a whole – undramatic, understated, yet with an exceptionally rich history and a

Steam-driven MS *Hjejlen* plies Lake Julsø, in the Lake District, during the summer months

calm, peaceful allure. This is a region of placid lakes, serpentine rivers and forested hills lying to the west of Århus in west Jutland. At the heart of the region is **Himmelbjerget** (literally the 'Sky Mountain') the highest point in Denmark at just 147m above sea level. It can be reached by road from the nearby town of **Ry**, which is the regional centre for such outdoor activities as cycling, canoeing and hiking.

From the top of Himmelbjerget, there are panoramic views over the hills and lakes. A winding path leads down from the summit to a jetty on the long, narrow Lake Julsø, where MS *Hjejlen*, claimed as the world's oldest working

paddle steamer, calls on its summer lake cruises from Silkeborg, the lake district's main town.

Though modern and comparatively featureless, **Silkeborg** is worth visiting for its museum, where 'Tollund Man' (see page119) is the principal exhibit.

Silkeborg is 40km west of Århus. The tourist office (including the Lake District) is at Torvet 9 (tel: 86 82 19 11).

Silkeborg Kulturhistiriske Museum, Hovedgaardsen, Hovedgaardsvej 7 (tel: 86 82 14 99). Open: mid-April to mid-October, 10am–5pm daily; mid-October to mid-April, noon–4pm Wednesday, Saturday and Sunday . Admission charge.

Passengers take to the water in Lego boats

theme park created with some 40 million Lego bricks. With around 1 million visitors a year, this is Denmark's number one tourist attraction.

Among the most popular features are Pirateland, where Captain Roger can be joined in his secret cave for feasts and treasure hunts, a miniature train, leading into a mountain cavern full of gold diggers, and a Lego safari where a Zebra-striped jeep takes you through a savanna of life-sized elephants, giraffes, crocodiles and other wild animals.

At the Lego traffic school, children between 8 and 13 are given a 20-minute course in road safety as they learn to drive Lego cars, completing a course for which Legoland driving licences are issued. For younger children there are also Duplo (the larger-scale version of Lego) car and aeroplane rides. A monorail encircles the whole park and small electric self-drive boats carry their passengers down the Nile to Abu Simbel in Egypt, then to a Japanese emperor's palace, by way of the Athenian Acropolis and New York's Statue of Liberty.

The attention to detail is amazing in the reproductions of Copenhagen's

LEGOLAND

The story of Legoland started with an unemployed Danish carpenter in the 1930s. He began to make wooden toys which he called Lego – the Latin for 'I play', which also cleverly combines the Danish words *leg godt*, meaning 'play well'. In 1947 he opened his first factory making plastic bricks. In 1968, with Lego by now a global phenomenon, Legoland Park opened at Billund.

There are thought to be roughly 300 million Lego engineers around the world. Of these, many would consider that playing with the world-famous coloured bricks, would be the ultimate dream job for when they grow up. However, this privilege belongs to just a handful of designers who are responsible for building the features at Legoland – the

Amalienborg Castle, Amsterdam's Canal Circle, Austria's Tyrol region, and 'Medbourne', a fictitious English town combining elements from Stamford, Chester and York.

In the Indoor Collection there are swimming-pool-sized pits of Lego and Duplo to play with, Titania's Palace, a vast (non-Lego) palace with over 3,000 miniature pieces in 18 rooms, and a huge collection of antique toys.

Legoland is 10 minutes' walk from the arrivals terminal at Billund airport.

Legoland Park, Billund (tel: 75 33 13 33). Open: April to end-September daily. The much smaller Indoor Collection remains open from the third Sunday in September until mid-December. Admission charge.

The amazing world of Legoland is undoubtedly Denmark's major tourist attraction

MARIAGER FJORD

Denmark's longest fjord snakes into the eastern side of Jutland between Århus and Aalborg. Lined by wooded slopes and meadows that sweep down to the water's edge, this is an area popular with cyclists, walkers, sailors and windsurfers.

Enchanting Mariager village, on the south bank of the fjord, is worth visiting simply to wander the cobbled streets of yellow, half-timbered cottages leading down to the marina. There is a small museum displaying local archaeological finds and exhibits explaining 18th-century life in the town. Little remains of 15th-century Mariager Abbey, though some beautiful frescos survive in the church.

Mariager is 45km north of Århus. The tourist office is at Torvet 1B (tel: 98 54 13 77).
Museum, Kirkegade 4A (tel: 98 54 12 87). Open: mid-May to mid-September 11am–5pm.

RANDERS

Randers, Denmark's sixth largest city (with a population of around 60,000), straddles the River Gudenå in East Jutland. The modern industrial town has a thriving cultural life, and supports its own symphony orchestra. A modern concert hall and theatre have been constructed in a former power station known as the Værket.

Randers' history can be traced to the 11th century when rebels opposing Saint Knut are recorded as having met here. In the Middle Ages this was a thriving trading port with access to the sea via the Gudenå. Many fine old houses survive in the central shopping areas around Brødregade, Storegade, Houmeden and Rådhusstræde.

Randers' Kulturhuset (Cultural Centre) contains the city's two main museums. The **Randers Kunstmuseum** (Randers Art Gallery) has an excellent collection of contemporary Danish art, including work by Lundstrøm, Søndergaard and Jorn. The **Kulturhistorisk Museum** (Cultural History Museum) traces the development of Danish culture from early drawings and artefacts, through to 20th-century creations.

Randers is 36km north of Århus. The tourist office is at Tørvebryggen 12 (tel: 86 42 44 77).

RIBE

Rising out of the flat, marshy wetlands south of Esbjerg, and claimed as Denmark's oldest town, Ribe's history dates back to AD800 when it was a Viking trading settlement. Before the Reformation (1536) there were no fewer than nine abbeys and 13 churches here, as well as many other Catholic institutions. Most were closed, and a combination of fires, floods and plague, plus the silting up of the River Å, further reduced the town's eminence.

Today Ribe remains a small and beautifully preserved medieval town, with hundreds of half-timbered houses lining its ancient cobbled streets. The sight not to be missed is the cathedral, whose spire and tower are visible from a long way off. Construction work began in about 1150, with numerous subsequent rebuildings and additions. Inside, grey Romanesque arches contrast with the bright white walls, and there are monuments to various historical figures. From the top of the 14th-century tower there are expansive views over the marshes and tidal flats.

Ribe – one of Denmark's most important trading centres during the Middle Ages
Inset: the town's night watchman

Ribe is 30km southeast of Esbjerg. The Tourist Office is at Torvet 3–5 (tel: 75 42 15 00).

Ribe Domkirke, Torvet (tel: 75 42 06 19). Open: October to April, 11am–3pm Monday to Saturday and 1–3pm Sunday; May to September, 10am–6pm Monday to Saturday and noon–6pm Sunday. Admission charge

RINGKØBING

The old market town of Ringkøbing stands on the northern shore of the wide, calm Ringkøbing Fjord – the lagoon that is linked to the North Sea by a narrow neck of water at Nymindegab, at its southern tip. Founded as a trading port in the 13th century, Ringkøbing remained an important seafaring town until this channel silted up in the 18th century.

Access to the sea was severely limited until 1931, when locks were built at Hvide Sande, breaching the narrow spit of land and opening the fjord again. Even so, the fishing boats that land their catch at Ringkøbing harbour mainly operate on the fjord. A daily fish auction takes place in the new red wooden building at the harbour's edge, starting at 9.30am.

The **Ringkøbing Museum** (*tel: 97 32 16 15*) has a good collection of local archaeological and historical finds, and an excellent exhibition charting Mylius-Erichsen's exploration of northeast Greenland between 1906 and 1908.

Ringkøbing is 81km north of Esbjerg. The tourist office is at Torvet (tel: 97 32 00 31).

Tracks of a lone walker across the sand dunes at Råbjerg Mile, southwest of Skagen

SÆBY

This delightfully quaint and peaceful fishing village, situated on Jutland's northeastern coast, was the site of a large 15th-century Carmelite monastery. A long and extraordinarily narrow church is all that survives of the monastery, which has a magnificent 16th-century Dutch altarpiece; how it reached Sæby remains a mystery. The walls are bedecked with striking murals, including one depicting the devil taking the soul of a dead man while his widow is being comforted by her lover. Perhaps even stranger is the sign at the church entrance that pleads: 'Please don't bring ice cream, sausages and dogs into the church'.

Sæby is 45km northeast of Aalborg. The tourist office is at Krystaltorvet 1 (tel: 98 46 12 44).

SKAGEN

Flung far out on the tip of Jutland's fingernail, Skagen is one of the treats of touring the Danish countryside. The Skaggerak and Kattegat Seas – parts of the North Sea and the Baltic respectively – confront each other at this point in a perpetually churning commotion. The precise meeting point is at the end of a sand spit at **Grenen** 3km north of the town, where the road finally peters out. You can walk out along the spit, and put a foot in each sea as gales blow from both directions. It is a rare instance of elemental drama in otherwise placid Denmark.

Artists started settling in Skagen from the 1870s onwards, drawn by the rawness of the scenery and atmosphere, and by the startling clarity and brightness of its light. The **Brøndums Hotel** became their meeting place, and remains one of the main landmarks in this Bohemian little town. Portraits of the various Skagen school artists, painted by one another, hang in the bar, the lounge and the dining room and are a good introduction to their work.

The **Skagens Museum**, opposite the Brøndums Hotel, houses an excellent collection of their work in an airy setting that allows them to be viewed at their best. P S Krøyer, Laurits Tuxen and Michael and Anna Ancher (her father owned the Brøndums Hotel) are probably the best known artists of the school. As well as landscapes capturing subtle changes of light at different times of day, other popular subjects are fishermen dragging boats ashore and people walking on the beach at sunset. One canvas is widely recognised as the finest ever to hail from the Skagen School: P S Krøyer's *Summer Evening on the South Beach at Skagen.*

Skagen is 102km north of Aalborg. The tourist office is at Sankt Laurentii Vej 22 (tel: 98 44 13 77).

Skagens Museum, Brødumsvej 4 (tel: 98 44 64 44). Open: June to August, 10am–6pm daily; September to May, 1–4pm Tuesday to Friday. Admission charge.

Nearby

Nowhere else in Denmark is there anything quite like the wild drifting sand dunes created by competing winds and sandstorms which rage across the northernmost tip of the country.

Signposted off Road 597 is the bald, Sahara-esque **Råbjerg Mile**, located 12km southwest of Skagen and the highest of the dunes. It started advancing inland from the coast at Kandestederne beach a few centuries ago, and is expected to block Road 40, currently the only one to and from Skagen, in about 150 years time.

SKIVE

This ancient little town on the Salling peninsula, now a busy tourist centre in summer, makes a good base for exploring the western end of the Limfjord (see page 124).

(see page 124)

In the town itself, the **Skive Museum** is worth seeing for its extensive collection of amber and pearls which has been found locally, and the **Vor Frue Kirke** (the Church of Our Lady) has a particularly beautiful vaulted and frescoed ceiling.

Skive is 26km northwest of Viborg. The regional tourist office is at Østerbro 7 (tel: 97 52 32 66).

Brave fishermen lost at sea are remembered at Skagen

SØNDERBORG

Travellers crossing by ferry from south Jutland to south Fyn should stop at Sønderborg, near the German Border, to visit one of the most important historical sites in Denmark, a battle site memorial with a singular atmosphere, not matched anywhere else in the country.

Overlooking the town are the Dybbøl Banke military earthworks, a windmill, and a memorial stone to the hundreds of soldiers who died in the Prussian wars of 1848 and 1864. Denmark lost a third of Jutland in these defeats, which finally marked the end of the Danish empire that had once ruled much of Scandinavia. The memorial is set in a solemn and strangely beautiful spot.

Sønderborg is 37km east of Padborg.

The tourist office is at Rådhustorvet 7 (tel: 74 42 35 55).

Tønder, near the Danish border, feels as Teutonic as it does Scandinavian

TØNDER

This pretty little market town, down in the southwestern corner of Denmark, near the German border, has a sleepy air, accentuated by the somnolent marshlands that stretch out to the north, south and west. The main pedestrianised shopping street (made up of Vestergade, Storegade and Østergade) is lined with well-preserved gabled houses, some of them bearing the coats of arms of wealthy 18th-century merchants.

Sixteenth-century **Kristkirken** (Christ Church) is worth seeing for its famous 17th-century rood screen. There are two museums: the **Tønder Museum**, in the 16th-century tower gatehouse, which charts the town's history, including the story of its lacemaking industry; and the **Sønderjyllands Kunstmuseum** (South Jutland Art Museum) with its collection of 19th and 20th-century Danish and German works.

Tønder is 44km west of Padborg. The tourist office is at Torvet 1 (tel: 74 72 12 20).

VEJLE

Vejle is a busy commercial and industrial port town in East Jutland. It also has a relaxed ambience, and is set in a beautiful region of gentle hills, forests, lakes, rivers and fjords.

The town, dating from the 12th century, rises fairly steeply from the harbour, with **Sankt Nikolai Kirke** (Saint Nicholas' Church) at the highest point; inside, you can view the body of an Iron Age woman, preserved in a peat bog and discovered in the 19th century (see page 118).

A winding street leads up to a restored windmill, where there is a small exhibition of milling over the centuries. In the same building as the tourist office, which is in a former merchant's house, is a good local history museum. The **Vejle Kunstmuseum** (Vejle Art Museum) has a large collection of mainly Danish 20th-century drawings, paintings and sculpture.

Vejle is 30km north of Kolding and 75km southwest of Århus. The tourist office is at Søndergade 14 (tel: 75 82 19 55).

VIBORG

Viborg is one of Denmark's oldest cities, dating to the 8th century AD. It stands at a strategically important crossroads in central Jutland, midway between the Søndersø and Nørresø lakes. From the 11th to the 17th centuries it was the place where Danish monarchs were chosen and where they received the oath of allegiance from their subjects. It later declined, partly because of lack of access to the sea and partly because of the shift of political power to Copenhagen.

Viborg was also an important ecclesiastical centre, which accounts for the great twin-towered cathedral dominating the town. Only the crypt remains of the 12th-century church; after the ravages of fire and two centuries of neglect, the original building was demolished in 1863, and work on a huge new granite cathedral began the following decade. The interior is decorated with dazzling frescos by Joakim Skovgaard. The candelabrum in front of the choir is also noteworthy.

Viborg is 81km south of Aalborg. The tourist office is at Nytorv 5 (tel: 86 61 16 66).

Viborg Domkirke, Domkirkepladsen, Sankt Mogensgade 4 (tel: 86 62 11 07). Open: April, May and September, 11am–4pm daily; June to August, 10am–5pm daily; October to March, 11am–3pm daily. Admission free.

Political power left Viborg long ago, but the cathedral's twin towers still keep watch

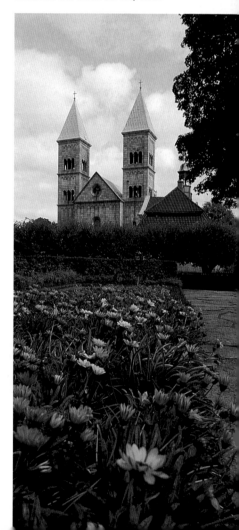

Århus

*W*ith a population of around 261,000, Århus is Denmark's second city and the cultural capital of Jutland. Originally a Viking port and trading centre, it burgeoned in the 13th century when the cathedral was begun, fell into ruins two centuries later, and recovered in the 16th century when many of the city's fine buildings were constructed. The old and new blend harmoniously in Århus, which has some exemplary modern architecture and an atmospheric old town where a large and lively student community thrives.

DEN GAMLE BY (THE OLD TOWN)

This is one of the best open-air museums in Denmark, with 70 reconstructed houses from all over the country set around a lakeside park. The purpose of the site is to demonstrate Danish village life from the 16th century through to the present, by recreating domestic and working scenes down to the last detail. There are potters, blacksmiths and carpenters, all in period dress, busy at their workshops, as well as homes with displays of toys, textiles, watches and china. All that's missing for real authenticity is the traditional smell!
Viborgvej (tel: 86 12 31 88). Open: January, February, March and November, 11am–3pm daily; April and October, 10am–4pm daily; June, July and August, 9am–6pm daily; December, 10am–3pm Monday to Saturday and 10am–4pm Sunday. Admission charge.

DET DANSKE BRANDVÆRNS MUSEUM (THE DANISH FIREFIGHTING MUSEUM)

This rare collection consists of almost 100 beautifully preserved vintage fire engines and pumps which tell the story of the evolution of equipment from handpumps, through horse-drawn fire engines, to the latest in fire-fighting technology.
Tomsagervej 25 (tel: 86 25 41 44). Open: June to September, 10am–5pm daily; October to June, 10am–5pm Tuesday to Sunday. Admission charge.

DOMKIRKE (CATHEDRAL)

Århus Cathedral – otherwise known as the Church of Saint Clement – is the longest church in Denmark, with a 93m nave. The awesome interior has 15th-century frescos by numerous different masters and the vast altarpiece is one of the most ornate anywhere in the country.

The structure dates from the early 13th century, when a Romanesque church was built on the site. Four chapels off the chancel, and a few other portions, survive, but much of it was destroyed by fire. Much of today's Gothic cathedral dates from the rebuilding of 1450 to 1520.
Bispetorvet (tel: 86 12 38 45). Open: October to April, 10am–3pm Monday to Saturday (except public holidays); May to September, 9.30am–4pm daily. Admission free.

FORHISTORISK MUSEUM MOESGÅRD (MOESGÅRD PREHISTORIC MUSEUM)

Set in an 18th-century manor house in the Moesgård woods, 5km south of the city centre (see page 120), this is Denmark's most extensive and absorbing museum. Various periods in Denmark's prehistory (up to and including the Viking era) are illustrated by archaeological finds. One of the star attractions is the leathery corpse of 'Grauballe Man' (see page 118) and among the Viking exhibits are swords and coats of mail, of which reproductions have been made for visitors to handle and wear. There is also an interesting exhibition on the

ethnography of Greenland (see page 134). *Moesgård Prehistoric Museum, Moesgård Allé 20, Højbjerg (tel: 86 27 24 33). Open: May to mid-September, 10am–5pm daily; mid-September to April, noon–4pm Tuesday to Sunday. Admission charge. Bus No 6 (Moesgård).*

Århus Tourist Office, Rådhuset (tel: 86 12 16 00).

ÅRHUS TOWN PLAN

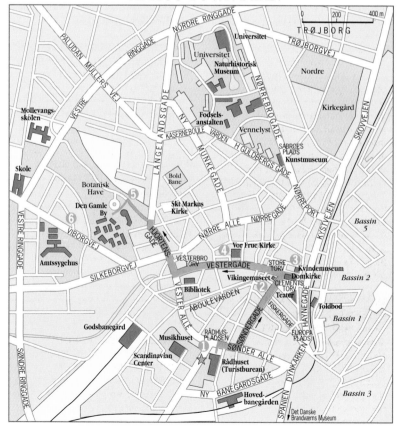

KUNSTMUSEUM (MUSEUM OF ART)

The city's art museum houses an excellent collection of Danish paintings, drawings and sculpture, ranging from the 18th century to the present day, supplemented by works from Germany and the United States. There are also regular exhibitions of emerging artists.

Vennelystparken (tel: 86 13 52 55). Open: 10am–5pm Tuesday to Sunday. Admission charge.

MUSIKHUSET ÅRHUS (CONCERT HALL)

The Århus concert hall is one of Denmark's principal centres for the performing arts and home to the Århus Symphony Orchestra, the Danish National Opera and the Århus Festival. Built in 1982, it is both elegant and highly functional, having been acclaimed internationally for its fine acoustics. There are two modern auditoriums, one of them with seating for over 1,000, and an airy foyer with plate-glass walls in which direct sunlight and indoor trees create an almost tropical effect.

Ballet and opera performances, as well as classical and modern concerts, are held regularly in the main auditoriums, and exhibitions of art in the foyer. Even if there is little going on, the concert hall is well worth visiting simply as an architectural sight.

Thomas Jensens Allé (tel: 86 13 43 44). Open: 11am–9pm daily, or later when performances are being held. Admission free, except to performances.

NATURHISTORISK MUSEUM (THE NATURAL HISTORY MUSEUM)

The museum features some beautifully arranged dioramas of Danish wildlife in authentic settings, as well as fauna from other parts of the world. There is also an interesting exhibition showing the influences which have shaped the Danish landscape since the Ice Age.

Bygning 210, Universitetsparken (tel: 86 12 97 77). Open: July and August, 10am–5pm daily, September and June, 10am–4pm daily; October to April, 10am–4pm Tuesday to Saturday. Admission charge.

The state-of-the-art Århus concert hall is an architectural wonder

St Clement's Cathedral at Århus is the longest in Denmark

RÅDHUSET (CITY HALL)

The City Hall is frequently described as an example of Danish design and architecture at its best. Modern, functional and clad in Norwegian marble, it is the work of Arne Jacobsen and was completed in 1941. The council chamber and civic hall are decorated with murals from the Nazi occupation, into which the artists slipped cryptic symbols of protest. The most striking feature is the 60m tower, from which there are superb views over the city.

Rådhuspladsen (tel: 89 40 20 00). Guided tours in English, German and French, including the bell tower, are conducted at 4pm on Monday to Friday all year. The tower only is open June to September, noon–2pm daily. Admission charge.

STENO-DANMARKS VIDENSKABSHISTORISK MUSEET (THE STENO MUSEUM))

This unusual and captivating museum, dedicated to the history of science and medicine, opened in 1994. A series of separate exhibitions begins on the ground floor with a collection of instruments used in astronomy, surveying, optics, magnetism, atomic and nuclear physics, chemistry, radio and computing – from Stone Age times, through the experimental physics of the 17th century, to the present day. Also on the ground floor is a parallel exhibition, charting the evolution of medicine from Hippocrates, in ancient Greece, through the invention of anaesthetics and X-ray, to a modern operating theatre.

Upstairs, a medicinal herb garden has been laid out on an outside terrace, based on herbs and substances described by Hendrik Smid in his 1546 *En Skjøn Lystig ny Urtegaard* (*An Attractive New Herb Garden*). The museum also has a planetarium, with shows at varying times on particular astronomical subjects. Some shows are specifically for children.

C F Møllers Alle 2, Bygning 100, Universitetsparken (tel: 89 42 39 75). Open: July and August, 10am–5pm daily; September and June, 10am–4pm daily; October to April, 10am–4pm Tuesday to Saturday. Admission charge.

PEAT MEN

A group of peaceful peat-cutters from Grauballe (32km west of Moesgård) got the shock of their lives one Saturday afternoon when one of them struck a human head topped with reddish hair about half a metre below the surface. As they unearthed more of the naked body, they found, to their horror, that its throat had been slit from ear to ear.

At first, a recent murder was suspected. An autopsy was conducted by a professor of forensic medicine from Århus university. Fingerprints were taken by the Criminal Investigation Department. A dentist examined the corpse's 20 remaining teeth. The most revealing analysis, however, was the carbon-dating which revealed the body to be approximately 2,000 years old.

Because of the peat's chemical composition, the body had lain in a state of perfect preservation. According to the professor its skin had undergone 'a process ... which appears to resemble most closely a tanning.' Between them, the experts managed to ascertain that the victim had been

'Grauballe Man' (opposite page) and 'Tolland Man' (above and left) rest in peace – as they have for the past 2,000 years or so

Moesgård Museum near Århus (see page 114) where he lies appearing to grin at his fascinated 20th-century visitors.

about 1.8m tall, and in his late thirties at the time of his death. He was also unused to manual work. He had probably been hit on the head and stripped naked before having his throat cut and being thrown into the bog. His last meal had been mainly of grain, although there were also traces of meat. He also suffered from intestinal worms.'Grauballe Man', as he is known, is now the star attraction at the

There were few clues to explain the motive for his killing, but his case is not unique. Several other bodies, including 'Tollund Man' have been discovered in the Jutland peat; many have met violent deaths. 'Tolland Man' died by strangulation, perhaps as a sacrificial victim, in about 220BC and, like 'Grauballe Man', was preserved in a peat bog before being discovered in 1950.

Moesgård

Moesgård is 5km south of Århus. This walk starts at the Prehistoric Museum and follows the so-called Prehistoric Trackway through a beautiful forest where ancient buildings have been reconstructed. *Allow 2 hours.*

1 FORHISTORISK MUSEUM MOESGÅRD (MOESGÅRD PREHISTORIC MUSEUM)

See page 114.

Follow the path that leads to the right of the museum (see page 114), through gardens, past a lake on the left and through an apple orchard, into the open field of Monument Park.

2 MONUMENT PARK

The park is strewn with reconstructed prehistoric burial chambers and other monuments from all over Denmark, which, for varying reasons, have had to be moved from their original sites. Many of these are cist tombs, covered with slabs of stone, including the large and imposing Stone Age Kobberup Cist, the only one of its kind ever found. The sheep, goats and ponies wandering the park are rare breeds closely related to those kept by the prehistoric inhabitants of Denmark.

From Monument Park a metalled road, shaded by beech, oak, ash and lime trees, leads down to the Skovmøllen.

3 SKOVMØLLEN (MILL)

The beautifully half-timbered watermill has been turned into a restaurant serving traditional Danish food, as well as bread baked with home-ground flour. Ask inside to be shown the chunky old machinery, restored and functioning perfectly as the Giber Å (river) turns the wheel which grinds the grain.

Past the mill, turn left on to a footpath that passes a dolmen on the

Lucky visitors to the Viking Town are treated to homemade bread, baked to an authentic recipe

right before entering and winding through the densest part of the forest. The trail emerges in an open field where the Tustrup temple stands.

4 TUSTRUP (HUSET) TEMPLE

Dating from about 2500BC, this Stone Age structure is thought to have been used for religious rituals, with gifts of food brought to appease the spirits of the dead. The temple was discovered and excavated in 1954 at Tustrup, about 80km north of Moesgård.

The path joins a trackway along the edge of the beach. Turn left and follow this trackway to the fisherman's house at the mouth of the Giber å (river). Turn left again, following the path that crosses to the north bank, via a footbridge, and leads to the Iron-Age House.

5 IRON-AGE HOUSE

This is a faithful reproduction of a house from the early Iron Age, constructed on the basis of a hut that was found at Tofting, just across the Danish border in Germany. The roof is supported by oak trunks, with shelter for the family at one end (next to a fire) and for their livestock at the other.

Immediately behind the house is an underground storage cellar, based on a similar one excavated at a different site, at Grønheden in north Jutland.

A footpath leads across a field back towards the Moesgård museum. Just beyond is the Viking Town.

6 VIKING TOWN

The reproduction Viking dwellings assembled here are based on those known from excavations in various regions of Denmark. The main exhibit is the Hedeby House, which has a working oven; visitors are sometimes offered a taste of homemade bread, with a swig of mead served in a stone cup.

Moesgård Prehistoric Museum,
Moesgård Allé, Højbjerg (tel: 86 27 24 33). Open: May to mid-September, 10am–5pm daily; mid-September to April, noon–4pm Tuesday to Sunday. Admission charge.

Aalborg

This stroll through old Aalborg starts at the heart of the city and takes in some historical sights before ending down at the fjord-side castle. *Allow 2 hours.*

Start in Gammel Torv.

1 RÅDHUSET

The square in front of the town hall is the oldest part of the city. Distances from Aalborg are still measured from the stone column in the middle. The Rådhuset itself is not the same building that Jens Bang so famously sneered at (see page 91) as this graceful yellow rococo edifice was not completed until 1762. Note the original gas lamps on either side of the entrance.

The façade of Jens Bang's house with the famous protruding tongue is opposite. Cross the square and follow the sign to the cathedral.

2 BUDOLFI DOMKIRKE

If you are here on the hour you will hear the carillon play (see page 91).

Pass the post office to the west of the cathedral, then turn down an alley leading into Adelgade. Turn right and follow the road into C W Obels Plads. On the square is the Helligåndsklostret.

3 HELLIGÅNDSKLOSTRET (MONASTERY OF THE HOLY GHOST)

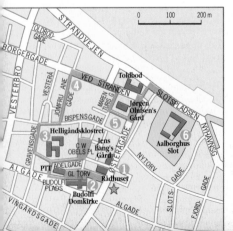

This former monastery is the oldest social institution in Denmark, dating from 1431. It was dedicated to the care of the elderly and infirm, and is still a home for 30 senior citizens. The conducted tour takes in a gloriously frescoed chapel and the monastic refectory.

Return to Adelgade, following the road down into the narrow and picturesque Latinergyrden (alley), emerging into pedestrianised Gravensgade. Turn right and right again at the end of the road into Bispensgade, then second left into Jomfru Ane Gade.

4 JOMFRU ANE GADE

This street is famous for its restaurants and cafés. There are about 30 in a 200m stretch and there is always a great atmosphere here. If it is not lunch time, at least make this a beer or coffee stop.
Turn right into Ved Stranden and right again into Maren Turis Gade. No 6 is Jørgen Olufsen's Gård. Go in through this entrance (the house itself is not open to the public).

5 JØRGEN OLUFSEN'S GÅRD

Built in 1616 by the wealthy Olufsen, (Jens Bang's brother, see page 91), there is probably no better-preserved merchant's house in Denmark. Note the hoists and doors to the grain lofts in the three-storey warehouse. In the gateway onto Østerågade, there is an original iron hook for weighing goods so that customers could check that they were not being cheated.
There is a second entrance on Østerågade. Exit the house here, turning immediately left, then right into the Slotspladsen, from where the castle comes into view.

6 AALBORGHUS SLOT (AALBORG CASTLE)

King Christian III built this castle in the 16th century as a defensive fortress, but it was never needed for that purpose and became the official residence of the Lord Lieutenant, and so it remains to this day. There is access only to the courtyard, ramparts and dungeon.

Aalborg Castle (tel: 98 13 45 11). Courtyard and ramparts open: 8am–sunset; dungeon and underground passage open: April to September 8am–3.30pm Monday to Friday. Admission free.

Monastery of the Holy Ghost (tel: 98 12 02 05). Guided tours are conducted from mid-June to mid-August at 2pm on Monday to Friday. On Tuesdays and Thursdays they are in English and Danish; on other days in German and Danish. Admission charge.

Many of the old merchants' houses in the town are now used as offices

Limfjord

The Limfjord cuts a slim slice through the tip of Jutland, dividing the south of the peninsula from its northern extremity, where the scenery becomes more rugged. This drive takes you round the splintering inlets and islands, through some of the wildest countryside in Denmark.
Allow 5 hours.

1 AALBORG

Aalborg (see page 90) was originally established as a Viking settlement, on account of its strategic position at the narrowest point on the Limfjord. The conurbation now straddles this stretch of water, together with its sister city Nørresundby on the northern side.
From central Aalborg follow the signs for Road No 187 towards Nibe, which is also called the Marguerite Route (see Driving on page 182). Stay on this route, following the brown and white daisy signs, to skirt the fjord, passing through Nibe and on to Løgstor.

2 LØGSTØR

The Limfjord Museum in the village demonstrates how closely the history of this town, as with others on the fjord, is entwined

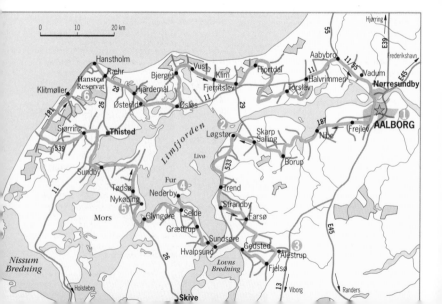

with the herring fishing industry, and with shipping and ferry traffic. The museum is in the former canal bailiff's house on the quayside facing on to the Frederik VII Canal. The canal was built to bypass a sandbar blocking one of the narrowest sounds on the Limfjord. *Continue along the Marguerite Route southwards, hugging the fjord, then turn sharply inland at Strandby, detouring to Ålestrup.*

Limfjord Museum, Kanalvejen 40 (tel: 98 67 18 05). Open: May to August, 10am–5pm daily; September and October, 2–5pm Tuesday to Saturday . Admission charge.

Jydske Rosenpark, Ålestrup (tel: 98 64 23 86). Open: June to mid-September, 10am–5pm daily. Admission charge.

Bicycle Museum, Borgergade 10 (tel: 98 64 19 60). Open: April to October, 10am–5pm daily. Admission charge.

---

nearby Mors island. Cliffs of clay rise above the Limfjord, and a museum in Nederby demonstrates how this geological oddity was formed. The fossils on display include that of a giant turtle. *Return to the Marguerite Route and follow it to the junction with Road No 26 from Thisted to Skive. Turn sharp right here and cross the bridge to Mors Island, turning right for Nykøbing.*

3 ÅLESTRUP

There are two good reasons to stop here. One is to see the **Jydske Rosenpark** (Jutland Rose Garden) featuring more than 15,000 blooms and 200 different species. The other attraction is the **Danmarks Cykelmuseum** (Bicycle Museum), displaying about 100 different machines, from boneshakers to the latest in mountain bikes. Although Denmark is noted for both museums and cycling, this place is unique in combining the two. *Stay on the Marguerite Route to Hvalpsund, from where the ferry to Sundsøre takes 10 minutes and gives wonderful views across the fjord. Continue north along the waterside, taking a detour off the Marguerite Route at Selde for the 5-minute ferry ride to Nederby, on Fur Island.*

4 FUR ISLAND

Fur is famous for its white clay, formed in part from fossilised algae and found nowhere else in the world except on

5 NYKØBING

Here you will find Dueholm Kloster (monastery), founded in 1370. The beautiful buildings house a historical museum charting the town's history. *Follow the Marguerite Route back over the bridge from Mors island and head for Thisted, by-passing the town and continue west until you reach the coast. Follow the coast road north to Hansted Game Reserve.*

6 HANSTED RESERVAT

This is Denmark's most extensive wilderness – a National Reserve of woodland, bogs and sand dunes rich in bird life and a stopping off point during the migratory season. During the breeding season it is forbidden to enter the reserve on foot (see page136). *The Marguerite Route returns to the fjord at Østerild, where you continue eastwards via Fjerritslev, Hjortdal and Torslev. At Halvrimmen leave the route to take Road No 11 back to Nørresundby and Aalborg.*

Århus

This walk takes you through the heart of Århus, taking in the historic centre of the town and some curious museums. For map, see page 115. *Allow 3 hours, not including time to explore Den Gamle By.*

1 RÅDHUSPLADSEN

Dominating Town Hall Square is the Rådhuset (see page 117). In the middle of the square is the large and amusing sculpture of a sow and suckling piglets, known as the Pig Fountain.

Walk down pedestrianised Søndergade, one of the city's main shopping streets, until it reaches Clementstorv (square). On the left is the Unibank building, with the Viking Museum in the basement.

2 VIKINGEMUSEET (VIKING MUSEUM)

When the foundations were being dug for the Unibank building in 1964, the remains of a Viking village's ramparts were discovered. Subsequently excavated, the site has been turned into a small museum showing a section of the original rampart and a reconstructed Viking home, complete with a loom, tools and utensils.

Outside the bank, turn right into Domkirkeplads, dominated by the great cathedral (see page 114). Next to the cathedral (at No 5) is the unusual Kvindemuseum.

Above street level in Århus

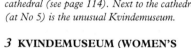

3 KVINDEMUSEUM (WOMEN'S MUSEUM)

The small museum, located in a former police station, illustrates the traditional everyday lives of women in Denmark, and charts the 20th-century progress towards equality.

Behind the cathedral is a warren of cobbled streets known as the Latin Quarter. This is an area of boutiques and curiosity shops, bubbling with café life, particularly in term time. After a brief exploration, return to Domkirkeplads. Pass the cathedral heading west to reach Store Torv, then continue straight on through Lille Torv and down Vestergade as far as the Vor Frue Kirke on the right.

The simple, elegant interior of the Church of Our Lady

4 VOR FRUE KIRKE (CHURCH OF OUR LADY)

This is the oldest structure in Århus, originally built by King Erik Ejegod in the 11th century. A former Dominican monastery, it survived the Reformation by instituting a hospital in the chapter house, which can be reached through a Gothic cloister. The nave is 14th century and the ornate altarpiece is 16th century. The real treat, however, is the vaulted crypt, which was only discovered during excavations as recently as the 1950s.

Continue down Vestergade and turn right at Vester Alle. Continue through Vesterbro Torv (square) and up Hjortensgade to entrance to the Botanical Gardens.

5 BOTANISK HAVE (BOTANICAL GARDENS)

This large area of parkland is strewn with exotic shrubs and flowers. There are also several glasshouses containing over 5,000 species of tropical and temperate plants.
Bear left through the gardens to the entrance to Den Gamle By (The Old Town).

6 DEN GAMLE BY

This is Denmark's most extensive and authentic reconstructed old town (see pages 114–15) and could easily absorb several hours of your time.

Viking Museum (tel: 86 27 24 33). Open: 9.30am–4pm Monday, Tuesday, Wednesday and Friday and 9.30am–6pm Thursday. Admission free.

Women's Museum (tel: 86 13 61 44). Open: mid-September to mid-May, 10am–4pm Tuesday to Sunday; June to mid-September, 10am–5pm daily. Admission charge.

Church of Our Lady (tel: 86 12 12 43). Open: May to August, 10am–4pm Monday to Friday and 10am–2pm Saturday; September to January, 10am–2pm Monday to Friday and Saturday 10am–noon; closed: Sunday. Admission free.

Fishing

As a maritime nation, with both North Sea and Baltic coastline, the history of the Danish people has always been bound up closely with fishing. Fish forms a substantial part of the Danish diet, whether fresh, frozen, smoked or soused. Fishing harbours punctuate the coastline. Some are huge ports such as Esbjerg, but many more are tiny villages where fishing boats bob side by side with gleaming white yachts and sailing dinghies. The romance of the fisherman's life has a special place in the Danish psyche; the old salt with a bushy ginger beard, puffing a pipeful of tobacco, is still to be found on many a quayside.

The hard facts surrounding fishing in the modern world, however, tell a rather different story. Fishing is now a massive global industry, over which nations frequently come to blows over quotas, traditional fishing rights and territorial waters. Denmark has one of Europe's largest fleets, with some 3,300 boats of varying size, manned by around 10,000 fishermen. As well as fishing the Baltic and the North Sea, large ships bring catches back from the North Atlantic.

Even though the Danes are great fish eaters, a full 90 per cent of the catch is exported, the bulk of it frozen or canned in giant fish-processing factories that can handle hundreds of thousands of tonnes annually of cod, plaice, mackerel and herring. In the same way as their counterparts working the land, Danish fishermen have rationalised their industry, specialising in a few products which satisfy world demand, while maintaining a semblance of the romance bound up in their history. For a fuller appreciation of this, it is well worth visiting the Fiskeri-Og Søfartsmuseet (Fisheries and Maritime Museum) at Tarphagevej in Esbjerg (see pages 96–7).

Fishing boats at Nørre Vorupor in Jutland

GETTING AWAY FROM IT ALL

'Save in England, where else
will you see so many acres of
brilliant green lush meadow.'
THOMAS COOK'S
Traveller's Gazette (1904)

The Faroe Islands

*T*he Faroes are among the most densely bird-inhabited islands in the world. Nobody knows quite what the population is, but the figure runs to teeming millions – many spending only the warmer months there, feasting on seafood, before flying back south in winter searching for warmer climes.

For the seabirds that constitute the majority of this population, the archipelago of 30 rugged rocky humps and soaring cliffs – stuck out in the wild north Atlantic, roughly half way between Shetland and Greenland – must be something approaching an avian heaven.

Guillemots, kittiwakes, razorbills, cormorants, fulmars, gannets, oystercatchers and great skuas are just a few of the scores of winged species that nest in the cliffs, dive for fish and plankton and strafe the rocks with their bright, white droppings. Colonies of comical puffins, with their multicoloured beaks are also regular visitors; however, some of the more sentimental among hundreds of bird watchers who visit the islands between April and August are upset by the netting, plucking and cooking of these rare delicacies to please the Faroese palate.

More controversial still is the subject of whaling. The annual slaughter of hundreds of pilot whales who come to feed around the Faroese shores, provokes arguments that are hard for visitors to ignore. 'Brutal' say many conservationists; 'we do it sustainably, as we have done for generations' counter the perpetrators. With the involvement of the likes of Greenpeace, the debate has taken on international proportions, and there are those calling for tourists to boycott the islands and find somewhere else to get away from it all.

However, fishing and fish processing,

not whaling or puffin-catching, is the mainstay of Faroese life. Eighteen of the islands are inhabited by a total of about 50,000 people. About 15,000 live in **Tórshavn**, the capital, on Streymoy, the largest island. There the busy little harbour features brightly painted houses and bobbing boats with pale blue hulls, moored alongside larger vessels that form part of a huge fishing fleet.

The rest of the island inhabitants are scattered around numerous coastal fishing villages or fjord-side settlements. A few live inland, farming the descendants of sheep brought to the islands by Irish monks in the 7th century. There are more than twice as many sheep as people on the islands, producing what some people believe to be the finest wool in the world.

A few other farmers struggle against the odds with arable crops, though only about 6 per cent of the land is cultivated. The rest is rocky, windswept and

---

Faroes tour operators
D&A Tours, Williamton House, Low Causeway, Culross, Fife KY12 8HL (tel: 01383 881700).
Regent Holidays, 31A High Street, Shanklin, Isle of Wight PO37 6JW (tel: 01983 864212).
For tourist information about the Faroes and Greenland, contact the Danish Tourist Board.

The port of Suderø on the island of Streymoy, home of a large Faroese fishing fleet

unyielding, and harassed by the islands' extraordinarily capricious climate. Without learning the lesson that the elements, not man, are boss it is very hard to enjoy the Faroes. Hiking expeditions, fishing trips and inter-island boat journeys happen not according to some carefully worked out timetable, but when the weather allows. Even so, sun, rain and mist frequently replace each other in the course of just a few minutes, resulting in constant changes to the Faroese scenery.

The landscape consists of majestic mountains and harrowing ravines, bald hills where scrubby grass is all that will grow and forbidding cliffs overlooking surf that crashes hundreds of feet below. Standing as near to the edge as you dare, you can feel the buffeting wind, smell the salty tang in the air and watch a shaft of golden light break through the mist, while listening to the screeching of a million seabirds and reflecting on our weakness and insignificance as a species in the face of nature.

ISLAND LIFE

Most Greenlanders and Faroese make their first trip to Denmark as children. Among the great excitements of arriving in the motherland from these far-flung reaches of the kingdom is the prospect of seeing trees. This is just one of the wonders which they have only previously read or been told about. Another is the commotion, noise and sheer scale of Copenhagen, which can induce utter bewilderment.

But emigration to sophisticated Europe is not a choice made by very many of these young people. A spell studying or a short period of work, perhaps; but most conclude that the quality of life is better where they grew up. Can there be beauty without icebergs? Do not big skies and buffeting winds beat high-rise blocks and traffic?

Underpinning these typical sentiments, however, is the fact that they can also make a very good living back home. The economies of both Greenland and the Faroes are based on fishing and fish-processing. By opting out of the European Union and its quotas they have maintained favourable trading conditions. In addition to this, there are large subsidies and entitlements to generous social security payments from Denmark, which

To the majority of Greenlanders and Faroese, the lure of the north and its unique way of life is irresistible

suffers pangs of national guilt about the colonial past and its impact on the local island culture.

Mercedes-Benz and BMW do good business in the Faroes. Greenland has only a few kilometres of road in total, but smart four-wheel drives are still commonplace. Fishermen and hunters come home to comfortable houses fitted with every modern convenience.

Supermarkets in the main towns are stuffed with imported food, clothing and consumer goods. You can buy everything from designer Italian clothes to exotic tropical fruits.

Inuit people in Greenland living at the extremities of human endurance, or Nordic communities in the Faroes – both are rare examples in the modern world of traditional lifestyles being lived in harmony with the developed world's new prosperity and security. Some say they are having their (fish) cake and eating it.

Greenland

*G*reenland cannot be described without recourse to superlatives. This largest of the world's islands, which history has made an autonomous part of the Kingdom of Denmark, could not be less like its green, gentle, distant and (comparatively) small motherland. For the sheer grandeur of nature and the sense of being at the globe's extremity, Greenland provides the ultimate in travel experiences.

In length, Greenland would stretch from Denmark to the Saharan desert; in width it could join Copenhagen to Moscow. More than 80 per cent of this vast land mass is blanketed by an ice cap up to 3km thick, leaving only rugged, fjord-indented coastal fringes uncovered. A scattering of hunting, fishing and fish-processing settlements make up the population of just 54,000.

The majority are brown-skinned, black-haired 'Inuit' people, following

lives based on ancient customs and speaking a language totally distinct from all others, save a few similarities with tongues spoken by their kith in Arctic North America and Siberia. Kalaallit Nunaat – Land of Man – is the Inuit name for their homeland.

Summer is the season for hiking, mainly in the south – which is the only region that gives any credibility to the country's English name. Though the ice cap is never far away, the treeless hills and valleys become lush, verdant and flecked with wild flowers. Shepherds make the most of the brief luxuriance, as they mind their woolly charges. Millions of seabirds screech around the cliffs, while seals dive and bask on the rocks. Natural historians come to spot musk oxen and arctic hares. Polar bears, however, rarely stray south of the frozen wastes.

Further north, around Disko Bay on the western coast, the world's bulkiest glacier flows off the ice cap. Every summer about 20,000 million tonnes of ice breaks off the Illulissat Icefjord to drift off down to the east coast of America. There is no better place than the settlement of **Illulissat**, which has a couple of small Scandinavian-style hotels, to view these icebergs by walking along

Uumannaq Island is icebound until the midsummer thaw

the cliffs, or by boarding the fishing boats that push their way along channels between the ice. Mastering a traditional seal hunter's kayak made of wood and hide, is another option, although extreme caution is needed in waters that are never far from freezing point.

The experience stretches the imagination to its limits. Brilliant white and turquoise-tinged skyscrapers, precipitous cliffs, cathedrals with soaring spires, alpine peaks, giant faces with hooked noses and thousands of other infinitely varied examples of nature's sculpture are strewn across the bay.

Left: Greenlandic sledge dogs harnessed in 'fan' formation
Above: an Inuit ice fishing

Earlier in the year, from March until May (before that, it is too dark) is the season for travelling by dog-sledge, with seal hunters. Before the thaw of the brief arctic summer, hunters and fishermen from Illulissat and Uumannaq (still further north) don their fur trousers and sealskin boots, harness their packs of fierce, slit-eyed Greenlandic sledge dogs (often called huskies, although actually a rather different breed) and set off across the sea ice or up frozen fjords. Recently, is has become possible for groups of intrepid tourists to join them.

Wielding the long and slimy sealskin whip, the first lesson involves delivering the shrill commands that keep the yelping, salivating dogs under control as they bound energetically across the ice. After drilling holes through the ice, dinner of dogfish and halibut can be caught on weighted lines, before spending the night in a tent pitched on top of a sledge with guy ropes pegged into the ice.

Greenland tour operators
Arctic Experience, 29 Nork Way, Banstead, Surrey SM7 1PB (tel: 01737 218800).

Nature Parks and Reserves

Draved Skov Nature Reserve

This reserve consists of an enchanting area of ancient broad-leafed woodland. Waymarked trails for hikers and cyclists meander through the lime, oak and elm trees whose stark winter beauty erupts with carpets of wildflowers in spring, before the dense, darkening foliage of summer arrives. For many, the best time to visit is mellow, russet-and-yellow autumn, when locals forage the forest for wild mushrooms.

About 70km south of Esbjerg in the southwestern corner of Jutland, near the German border.

Wigeon breed in Scandinavian wetlands and winter on the mudflats of southern Africa

Farum Nature Park

City-dwelling nature lovers escape from Copenhagen to wander among this park's footpaths or to spot the rich birdlife and flora.

20km northwest of Copenhagen.

Hansted Nature Reserve

This important breeding ground for wetland birds is enclosed between the North Sea coastal road and the Limfjord shore (see page 125). Although admired and enjoyed by many motorists, particularly in the busy summer holiday season, access to the reserve is forbidden during the breeding season. As well as marshes, the reserve encompasses sand dunes, open heathland and lakes.

Betweeen Klitmøller and Hantsholm in the far northwest of Jutland, beyond Limfjord.

Høje Møn Nature Park

The scenery on the island of Møn (see page 54) includes chalk cliffs that rise dramatically out of the sea to a height of 128m. This nature park includes the forests that blanket the east of the island, ending abruptly at the cliff tops. Hiking and cycling trails wind through the undergrowth.

On the easern tip of Møn.

Nekselø Nature Reserve

Nekselø is a tiny island, the whole of which is designated as a nature reserve. Boats make the short crossing from the small harbour of Havnsø throughout the summer. The island's meadows and lakes contribute to an atmosphere entirely different from the rest of Zealand.

120km from Copenhagen off Zealand's northwestern coast.

Rands Fjord Nature Park

Despite its name, this 'fjord' is a freshwater lake, owing its name to the fact that it was once connected to the sea on Jutland's eastern coast. Footpaths lead round the lake, which is an

Farum Nature Park provides a welcome respite from city life in Copenhagen 20km away

important staging point for several species of wading birds, while wildfowl breed in the reedbeds.
Southeast of Vejle (see pages 112–13), about 6km beyond Børkop, on the road to Fredericia.

Rebild Bakker Nature Park

This park comprises the core of the Rold Skov, the most extensive area of woodland in Denmark, covering around 80sq km. It is also the richest in wildlife, home to red deer, roe deer, foxes, squirrels and martens. Nocturnal visitors might spot a badger or, occasionally, a wild boar.

As one of the country's hilliest regions, there are numerous streams trickling down from the high ground to feed a scattering of lakes and small ponds. Some of the rarest flora in Denmark, including orchids not found anywhere else in the country, grow along their moistened banks.

By a curious quirk of history, this nature park owes its existence to a group of Danish-Americans whose parents emigrated in the 19th century. Wanting to keep their links with Denmark alive, they purchased a swathe of land in the Rebild hills (*bakker* is the Danish for hills) and presented it to the Danish people in 1912, on condition that it should remain a nature park forever.
About 25km south of Aalborg, on the road to Holbro.

Above: bird-watching near Randers
Left: wild deer roam free in many parks

however, is the sight of thousands of avocets arriving in July and August to breed before departing in the autumn. *Rømø island is joined to mainland Jutland via a 9km-long causeway built across the tidal mud and sand flats. It is reached by taking the A12 south from Esbjerg, and turning right for the causeway in the town of Skaerbaek.*

Skagen Nature Park

Up on the tip of Jutland, this is Denmark's wildest area, the point where the peninsula meets the Skagerrak and Kattegat seas. There is unrestricted year-round access to the park whose trails pass through wind-buffeted sand dunes, heathland and conifer forests. Skagen is also a key spot for observing migrating birds, especially between April and June when thrushes and finches fly northwards in huge numbers on their way to Norway and Sweden.
The park is reached by driving north from Aalborg as far as you can go, past Frederikshavn and Skagen.

Rømø Nature Reserve

Although only part of the island is designated as a nature reserve, the whole of Rømø enjoys an atmosphere of isolation and seclusion. To the north are grassy meadows and sand dunes that sweep in an arc down to the south. The central areas rise to heathland, while the eastern side, looking across the flats to mainland Jutland, is alive with migratory wading birds in the spring and autumn. The greatest treat for bird watchers,

Skallingen Nature Reserve

The views are best from the northern stretch of the peninsula, where, in autumn you look out over the wetlands to thousands of pairs of eider duck and dunlin, along with rarer pink-footed geese, greenshanks and (in summer) the occasional ruff.

Located on a 10km-long peninsula of marshes and sand dunes facing the North Sea, 20km west of Esbjerg and reached along a narrow road from the village of Ho.

Tipperne Nature Reserve

There is no public access to the central part of the reserve, although there is an information centre and observation tower (access restricted to 1–5pm on Wednesdays, Fridays and Sundays in June and July). There are also footpaths around the periphery where some of the birdlife can be observed. Dunlin and wigeon breed here in profusion, and, in winter, up to 5,000 pairs of Bewick's swans can arrive. To the south of the reserve is a popular hunting area; wildfowling is permitted from 15 October to early spring.

Located on a small peninsula at the southern end of the Ringkøbing Fjord. It can be reached by road from Esbjerg via Varde or Billum, turning right just before Nyminde.

Tistrup-Bavelse Nature Park

The woodlands and meadows of this extensive park are dotted with prehistoric monuments, as well as lakes and marshes where wildfowl breed in winter.

Located between Ringsted and Fuglebjerg in southwestern Zealand.

Utterslev Mose Nature Reserve

This shallow, marshy lake and its surrounding parkland is a haven of peace rich in birdlife, despite the road bridges (including a four-lane highway) that cross it. Water channels cut through the expanses of reeds and marsh where wildfowl nest; footpaths and cycle tracks skirt the perimeter.

6km from central Copenhagen. Buses 63 and 68 from Rådhuspladsen drop you within a couple of minutes of the reserve.

Wild Skagen Nature Park is buffeted by winds from the Baltic and North Seas

Remote Islands

Denmark comprises over 400 islands, and since the Danes are a nation of bridge builders, leading the world in bridge design and engineering, many benefit from fixed road links. Funen is linked to Jutland, for example, and Zealand is soon to be linked, in turn, to Funen. Bridges link both these islands to several smaller ones in their respective archipelagos. However, for a sense of true insularity, there remain a number of very remote islands whose inviolable isolation is part of their special charm.

Læso, out in the Kattegat Sea (1½ hours by ferry from Frederikshavn in North Jutland), is a tranquil haven of woodland and heath, sand dunes speckled with marram grass, salt marshes rich in wildlife and long, exposed beaches. The resident population is just 2,500, most of them living in the port of Vesterø Havn, where the ferry lands, or in Byrum, the main town.

Samsø, almost equidistant from Jutland, Zealand and Funen and accessible by ferry from the former two, is more densely populated than Læso, although roughly the same size. It is also a popular holiday isle for nature lovers who rent homes there to enjoy the beaches and to cycle through the forests and meadows.

Tiny **Anholt**, about halfway between Jutland and Sweden, bans all motor vehicles from its 22sq km, most of which consist of sand dunes, beaches and plains. Occupied by the British Navy during the Napoleonic wars (when it was known as HMS *Anholt*), the island has prospered in more peaceful times. The 150-strong population welcomes small numbers of visitors each summer, mainly as paying guests in their own homes, although there is one inn and one camp site. To reach the island involves a 2½-hour ferry journey from Grenå in east Jutland.

Læso, an island that appeals to 'Robinson Crusoe' types

DIRECTORY

'Other cities put up statues of generals and potentates.
In Copenhagen they give you a little mermaid.
I think that's swell.'

BILL BRYSON
Neither Here Nor There

Shopping

*D*enmark is no place for bargain-hunters. Instead, the joy of shopping in Copenhagen and other Danish cities is the range of high-quality goods on offer, presented in the style for which the country is famous. For serious purchases of the best in Danish design, your pocket needs to be deep; however, for substantial buys the pain can be alleviated by refunds of the 25 per cent Value Added Tax (see box opposite).

AMBER

Amber – fossilised resin – washes up on Baltic beaches and has been worked into jewellery by the Danes for centuries, being sold as earrings, necklaces and other trinkets all over Denmark.

CANDLES

Danes are incorrigible candle-burners, with flickering flames adorning every meal table, including breakfast. Appropriately, candle-making is

something of an art-form in Denmark and they come in all shapes, sizes and designs. Many department stores and gift boutiques stock a huge range of candles and candle holders in traditional and avant-garde designs. Both make excellent gifts or souvenirs.

CLOTHING

The latest in fashion is available in shopping malls and department stores in all Danish cities. Denmark is also a country in which you will find top-quality traditional couture, from hand-tailored suits for men and women, to leisurewear for the stylish and debonair.

Knitwear, especially woollen sweaters, is a Scandinavian speciality and good buys can be found all over Denmark. In increasing numbers of shops, traditional designs are being supplemented by brighter, highly imaginative patterns.

You may have to endure politically correct didactics if you wear Greenlandic **seal fur**, but you could salve your conscience by remembering that this trade supports traditional Inuit communities who practice traditional methods of sustainable hunting from which environmentalists could learn a lot. The fur is also beautifully soft.

Silverware is among the more expensive souvenir items that can be bought

Bric-à-brac galore in Copenhagen's flea markets, held during the summer months

GLASS

There are several modern Danish glassblowers who have combined their ancient craft with progressive design ideas. Holmegaard of Copenhagen, on Copenhagen's Østergade 15–17, is the most famous producer. There is a museum of glass in Ebeltoft (see page 96).

HI-FI EQUIPMENT

The ultra-sleek designs of Bang & Olufsen are among Denmark's most renowned exports. The company has centres displaying the latest equipment in several Danish cities; in Copenhagen they are at Østergade 3–5.

PORCELAIN

Royal Copenhagen and Bing & Grøndal are the two best-known names in Danish porcelain, both now belong to the same company, but maintain distinct styles.

Window shoppers eye jewellery in Copenhagen: usually an expensive commodity here

COPENHAGEN

The pedestrianised Strøget or 'Promenade' – actually five different but consecutive streets – is over 1km long and is the main shopping focus in the capital, with hundreds of outlets ranging from tawdry tourist boutiques to Denmark's most stylish shops. Here are a few which the shopping aficionado should not miss.

Birger Christensen

This is the place to view the fullest range of furs in Denmark, including a wide selection from Greenland. There is another branch at Copenhagen airport. *Østergade 38.*

Håndarbejdets Fremme

This is the headquarters of the Danish Handicraft Guild and it displays the best in Danish embroidery, including work designed by Queen Margrethe. There is also a good selection of ceramics, woodcarvings, jewellery and other handicrafts. For many items, prices are surprisingly low, making this an excellent place to hunt for gifts. *Vimmelskaftet 38.*

Hans Hansen Silver

Perhaps the best place in Denmark for intricately worked silver, ranging from traditional styles to artistry influenced by more modern trends. *Amergertov 16.*

Kaufmann

One of two places in Copenhagen (see Sweater Market opposite) stocking a good selection of Scandinavian hand-knitted sweaters and other wool garments. *Nygade 2–4.*

Rosenthal Studio-Haus

One of the most elegant shops in town with the latest in chic designer gear from Denmark, Paris and Milan. *21 Frederiksberggade.*

Royal Copenhagen Antiques

Porcelain by Royal Copenhagen and Bing & Grøndal, Holmegårde glassware, and silverware by the top Danish silversmiths, Georg Jensen and A Michelsen. *Amagertorv.*

Sweater Market
Stocks a huge range of hand-knitted Scandinavian pure wool sweaters in traditional and classical designs. Many come with matching accessories, such as caps, scarves, gloves and socks.
Frederiksberggade 15.

The Latin Quarter, west of the Strøget, abounds with shops selling a huge variety of cheap knick-knacks, books, toys, furniture, stamps, musical instruments, military medals and uniforms and furniture. East of the Strøget, is a series of streets lined with antique shops.

Other places for bric-a-brac – and sometimes for good-quality seconds, at far lower prices, of names such as Royal Copenhagen (porcelain) or Holmegårde (glass) – are the flea markets open throughout the summer. The best are on Israel Plads, by the main railway station, and Smallegade.

AALBORG
Lange Handicraffts
A city-centre shop with an old farmhouse atmosphere, selling good selection of stoneware, china and glass, and mounting handicraft demonstrations in its workshop.
Hjelmerstald 15.
Magasin
One of the largest department stores in Scandinavia. A shopper's paradise with just about everything.
Nytorv 24.

ODENSE
Inspiration
This is the place to find the widest selection of Danish handicrafts on Funen including Royal Copenhagen porcelain and Georg Jensen silverware.
Vestergade 82–84.

ÅRHUS
Bilka
If you are thinking big, make your way out of town to Denmark's largest hypermarket. Here you will find everything imaginable, from high quality to budget – 15,000sq m of shopping under one roof.
Agerøvej 7.
Salling
Top-quality department store, with 30 specialist shops under one roof, including jewellery, designer clothing, china, glass and handicrafts.
Søndergade 27.
Victoria
Selling a selection of chic Danish-designed clothing, plus accessories and jewellery.
Østergade 25–27.

Birger Christensen Furs are at the forefront of a controversial trade

DANISH DESIGN

If one company embodies the design pre-eminence that Denmark has claimed since the 1950s, it is Bang & Olufsen. The company's sleek, high-tech television sets and hi-fi equipment are in demand as status symbols all over the world. Significantly, the electronic components are made by Japanese firms. Denmark has chosen not to compete at the cutting edge of electronic innovation. What it does offer is a flair for design. The partnership with Japan allows Bang & Olufsen to combine design quality with technical excellence.

Furniture, glassware, porcelain, cutlery, jewellery, silverware, lighting and architecture are other areas in

which Danish designers have been setting world trends in recent decades. The explanation for this phenomenon

Top-quality design is a symbol of modern Denmark (above, left and bottom right)

probably lies in a combination of the highly developed crafts which already existed in Denmark before World War II, and a national mood after 1945, which looked forward in rather the same way that the defeated nations did, rather than resting on the laurels of victory and history.

Simplicity became a theme, as the functionalism of the pre-war years was combined with a

Above: revolutionary architecture at Tycho Brahe Planetarium

sense of aesthetics. Why should not everyday objects such as tables, chairs, knives and forks, for example, be both practical and beautiful? In many parts of Europe, especially Britain, the concept of beauty in design is still anchored to the concept of the antique, but Danish designers have bounded off into pastures new. Ironically, some of the classic Danish designs of the 1950s and '60s have now assumed a sort of 'antique' value of their own – enough for them to be collected and displayed in museums around the world.

Entertainment

COPENHAGEN

Copenhagen is the most vibrant city in Scandinavia, with an immensely varied year-round entertainment programme and a nightlife that ranges from the cosy to the throbbing, and which lasts until dawn. Throughout the summer, street entertainment is an inescapable feature of the city. Along the Strøget and elsewhere musicians – classical, folk and modern – as well as jugglers, acrobats and clowns lend Copenhagen a carnival atmosphere that can add to the enjoyment of drinking at the numerous outdoor cafés.

For listings of concerts and cultural events, get a copy of *Wonderful Copenhagen* or *Copenhagen This Week* from the tourist office. A full list of entertainment possibilities is published in *Copenhagen This Week* (also free from the tourist office) from the respectable to the raunchy. Live music is played in many venues, and jazz is particularly popular in the capital.

CINEMAS

New-release English-language films reach Denmark quickly; they are, almost invariably shown with the original soundtrack and Danish sub-titles. Listings are found in daily newspapers.

Grand

Esoteric and arty films for the trendy set. *Mikkel Bryggersgade 8 (tel: 33 15 16 11).*

There is no lack of entertainment in Copenhagen, from Palads movie theatre (below) to Daddy's disco (right)

Imperial
Worth going to see anything here just for the experience of viewing the vast screen, which some say is the largest in Europe.
Vesterport Station (tel: 33 11 82 32).

Palads
A large complex with several different screens, often showing the newest releases.
Alex Torv 9 (tel: 33 13 14 00).

CLASSICAL MUSIC
Radiohusets Koncertsal
The main venue for classical concerts.
Julius Thomsensgade 1 (tel: 31 10 16 22).

DISCOS
Copenhagen is at the heart of European youth culture, on the pulse of the latest musical trends.

Annabell's
Pricey, up-market and generally avoided by teenagers.
Lille Kongensgade 16 (tel: 33 11 20 20).

Axels Dansebar
Energetic, fast-moving disco.
Scala, Alex Torv (tel: 33 11 19 15).

Daddy's
Respectable, with an older clientele.
Alex Torv 5 (tel: 33 11 46 79).

Exalon
Huge venue with three separate dance floors, each gyrating to different music.
Frederiksberggade 38 (on the Strøget) (tel: 33 11 08 66).

U-matic
Perhaps the trendiest place in town, with the latest beat.
Vestergade 10 in the basement of Krasnapolsky bar (tel: 33 32 88 00).

Copenhagen's Royal Theatre, where the opera and ballet seasons run from September to June

Woodstock
The place for '60s and '70s nostalgia.
Popular with thirty-somethings.
Vestergade 12 (tel: 33 11 20 71).

LIVE MUSIC
Bananrepublikken
The place for world music.
Nørrebrogade 13 (tel: 35 36 08 30).

Ca'Féen Funke
Fans insist its the best funk place in
town.
Sankt Hans Torv (tel: 31 35 17 41).
Café Pavillionen
Open-air rock concerts, great on a warm
evening, free of charge.
*Fælledparken, near Nørre Allé and
Tagensvej.*

Copenhagen Jazz House
Great atmosphere: Denmark's number
one jazz venue.
Niels Hemmingsengade 10
(tel: 33 15 26 00).
Country Rock Café
Mainly country and western.
Griffenfeldtsgade 20 (tel: 31 34 80 00).
Mojo
Good solid blues and rock.
Løngangsstræde 21c (tel: 33 11 64 53).
Rust
Noisy venue where many up-and-coming
rock bands make their names.
Guldbergsgade 8 (tel: 31 35 00 33).

THEATRE, OPERA AND BALLET
Det Kongelige Teater
Denmark's main opera and ballet venue,
plus theatrical performances.
Kongens Nytorv (tel: 33 32 20 20).
Kanonhallen
Theatre year-round, avant garde dance
and other cultural performances in the
summer.
Serridslevvej 2 (tel: 35 43 20 21).

OUTSIDE COPENHAGEN
The entertainment scene away from
Copenhagen pales in comparison with
the capital. Nevertheless, the night owl
will find lively nocturnal activities in the
university city of Århus, particularly in
term time, and in Odense and Aalborg.
All three also have their own symphony
orchestras.

AALBORG
Most of Aalborg's nightlife happens on
Jomfru Ane Gade, the vibrant,
pedestrianised street between Bispengade

and Borgergade, which is lined with
restaurants, cafés, bars and discos.
Aalborg Kongres og Kultur Center
The city's main music and culture centre
staging events of all kinds from boxing to
classical concerts.
Europa Plads 4 (tel: 99 35 55 55).
Fru Jensen
Live music every night, except Sunday,
in a cosy atmosphere.
Jomfru Ane Gade 13 (tel: 98 16 98 99).
Rock Nielsen
A popular disco which also stages
concerts, often featuring internationally
known rock bands.
Jomfru Ane Gade 9–11 (tel: 98 13 99 29).

Posters advertise 'what's on' in Tivoli Gardens,
Copenhagen

Open-air rock concerts are held regularly throughout the summer at the Café Pavillionen

Skråen

A café and multiscreen cinema that also features concerts by local bands.
Strandvejen 19 (tel: 98 12 21 89).

ESBJERG

Esbjerg's disco and live music scene is mostly to be found around Torvet, the main square.

Café Biografen

Café downstairs and live bands several nights a week in the room above.
Finsensgade 1 (tel: 75 45 09 22).

Esbjerg Teater

Stages Danish (and occasionally English) productions.
Komgensgade 34 (tel: 75 45 30 55).

You'll Never Walk Alone
An English-style pub with live bands.
Kongensgade 10 (tel: 75 45 40 60).

ODENSE
A local magazine called *Jam*, available free from the tourist office, lists the live-music action. Throughout the annual summer jazz festival there are free outdoor concerts.

Atlantic Night Club
Up-market disco playing the latest rock numbers.
Overgade 45–7 (tel: 65 91 05 27).

Badstuen
Musicians of alternative persuasion are usually to be found in this radical haunt.
Østre Stationvej 26 (tel: 66 13 48 66).

Boogies
Popular dance spot beneath Birdies café.
Nørregade 21 (tel: 66 14 00 39).

Café Oscar
A wide variety of musicians, including folk singers.
Vestergade 75 (tel: 66 14 25 35).

Cotton Club
Another good jazz venue.
Pantheonsgade 5 (tel: 66 12 55 25).

Dexter
Lively bar with buffet food and live jazz.
Vindegade 65 (tel: 66 13 68 88).

Musik Koelderen
The most popular jazz and blues venue in Odense.
Dronningensgade 2b (tel: 65 91 40 60).

Rytmeposten
Loud music from mainly local rock bands in this converted post office.
Østre Stationvej 27a (tel: 66 13 60 20).

Multihuset
The city's principal music venue, staging all kinds of concerts, from rock to classical and jazz.
Gasværksgade 2 (tel: 75 18 00 00).

Strandbio
Five-screen cinema showing recent English-language releases.
Strandbyplads 7 (tel: 75 12 15 07).

ÅRHUS
For listings get a copy of *Århus – A City For All Ages*, plus the monthly *What's on in Århus*, free from the tourist office.

Århus Teater
This old-established theatre has four
separate stages – a main one where
classical drama is performed, and three
smaller ones for fringe performances.
Bispetorvet (tel: 86 12 26 22).

Bent J
Small lively jazz bar that stays open late.
Nørre Allé 66 (tel: 86 12 04 92).

Blitz
Very trendy disco. Rock music on three
separate dance floors.
Klostergade 34 (tel; 86 19 10 99).

Downtown
Mainly rock. Popular with students.

Scanning the billboards to see where it's at

Store Torv (tel: 86 13 95 77).

Eiffel
Rock music. Open till dawn.
Store Torv 11 (tel: 86 20 15 66).

Fatter Eskil
Mainly blues but sometimes more
modern jazz bands.
Skolegade 25 (tel: 86 12 79 45).

Glazzhuset
The city's largest and principal jazz club.
Clemensborg (tel: 86 12 13 12).

Music Café
Occasionally mounts experimental fringe
theatre performances.
Mejlgade 53 (tel: 86 19 22 55).

Musikhuset Århus
The city's magnificently stylish concert

The Groennegaards Theatre (above and right) specialises in classical Danish drama. It lies off Kongens Nytorv in the centre of Copenhagen

hall stages a wide variety of classical concerts year round, plus opera, jazz, rock bands and other forms of entertainment.

Thomas Jensens Allé (tel: 86 12 12 33).

Palace

The city's principal cinema, with four screens, showing recent English-language releases.

Tordenskjoldsgade 21 (tel: 86 16 83 00).

Vestergade 58

Atmospheric folk and jazz club, sometimes also featuring guest rock bands.

Vestergade 58 (tel: 86 13 02 17).

Children

Children are well catered for all over Denmark, with a wide variety of activities available to suit all ages. Many museums and tourist attractions have a play area or a special exhibition for youngsters. These keep children amused so that their parents get the most out of their sightseeing. Similarly, hotels and restaurants nearly all have cots, high chairs and special menus. The one ingredient that parents might find lacking is a sense of warmth towards children. Every juvenile need is catered for, but Danish reserve is such that children are rarely made a fuss of.

ACTIVITY PARKS

'Sommerlands' parks are to be found in many parts of Denmark – commercially run parks offering a wide variety of water and land-based activities, such as water chutes, water cycles, rafts, pony rides, go-carting and shooting ranges.
Contact tourist offices for information.

LEGOLAND

This is undoubtedly one of the best children's attractions in the world (see page 106).

SAFARI PARK

Knuthenborg Safari Park, on the island of Lolland, features more than 900 animals from around the world. There is also a small zoo especially for young children.
Knuthenborg Safari Park, Godskontoret, Birketvej 1, DK-4941 Bandholm (tel: 53 88 80 88). Open: May to September 9am–6pm daily. Admission charge.

TIVOLI FRIHEDEN

This large amusement park is located near the centre of Århus and is set in a beautiful park. Open-air concerts in summer.
Skovbrynet, Århus (tel: 86 14 73 00). Open: July and August, 1–11pm daily: June, 1–10pm daily. Admission charge.

TIVOLI GARDENS

No trip to Copenhagen is complete without a visit to Tivoli Gardens which are particularly thrilling for children, and especially at night (see page 40).

Great fun for all the family at Tivoli World, North Jutland

Wow! Exhibits at the veteran car museum in the grounds of Aaholm Castle near Nysted, Lolland

TIVOLI WORLD
The largest amusement park in North Jutland. A large fun fair within a walk of the city centre with harrowing rides and popular fairytale figures wandering around.
Aalborg (tel: 98 11 12 55). Open: April to June, 1–8pm daily; July and August, 10am–10pm daily. Admission charge.

VANDLAND AQUACENTRE
The largest, indoor aquatic centre in northern Europe with water slides, wave machines, a 'Captain's Fun Land' and a 'Pirates' Play Land'.
Bilka, Vandmanden 5, Aalborg (tel: 98 18 92 00). Open: 11am–9pm Monday to Friday, 10am–9pm Saturdays and 10am–8pm Sundays. Admission charge.

ZOOS

Aalborg
Good open spaces (for both animals and visitors) in this imaginatively sculpted landscape.
Mølleparkvej 63 (tel: 98 13 07 33). Open: 9am–6pm daily. Admission charge.

Copenhagen
Good selection of animals, a special mini-zoo for small children and a new Tropical Zoo.
Roskildevej 32 (tel: 36 30 20 01). Open: November to March, 9am–4pm daily; April to May, 9am–5pm Monday to Friday and 9am–6pm weekends; June to October, 9am–6pm daily; September and October, 9am–5pm daily. Admission charge.

Sport

*D*anes are keen sports players and spectators, with a particular passion for football. The recent success of the Danish national team, and the worldwide reputations of a handful of Danish players, have added to this. Two other sports in which Denmark is prominent are badminton and sailing. A wide variety of participant and spectator sports can be enjoyed by visitors to Denmark.

ANGLING

A licence must be obtained to fish in natural waters in and around Denmark. The licence is valid for a year, costs 100Dkr and can be purchased from Danish post offices or larger fishing-tackle shops. Weekly and daily licences

An angler enjoying a bit of solitude at sundown near Assens

are also available for 75Dkr and 25Dkr respectively. Those aged under 18 or over 67 are exempt from the licence.

Fishing rights in natural lakes and streams are almost invariably private, but are often let to local angling societies which issue day or week cards. In addition to the fishing licence described above, rates are around 20–40Dkr for a day card and 75–100Dkr for a week

card. In many places, boats can be rented with fishing rights included. Often, these cards are available from local tourist offices who also have details of the freshwater fishing possibilities in the area.

For sea fishing, nearly all stretches of Denmark's 7,500km of coastline are accessible to the public as long as there is a passable beach between the sea and cultivated land. The coast must be approached by a public road only. Anglers may not take up position within 50m of a public house. A licence is required as detailed opposite, but no other special permission is needed. For safety reasons, jetty fishing is prohibited at several places on the North Sea coast.

In many Danish harbours, fishing boats will take anglers out to sea for a reasonable charge. Larger groups can charter a boat for themselves. Sea-fishing tours are arranged throughout the year from Copenhagen, Helsingør, Korsør and Frederikshavn. From other harbours, there are usually tours in summer months only. A fishing licence, but no other form of permission, is needed.

Further information and addresses of local angling societies contact:
Danmarks Sportsfiskerforbund
Worsåesgade 1, DK-7100 Vejle
(tel: 75 82 06 99).

ATHLETICS

Athletics meetings are held in Denmark all the year round, and many of them are open to foreign entrants.

One of the best known annual events is the Copenhagen Marathon which takes place in May.

For further information contact:
Idrættens Hus, Brøndby Stadion 20, DK-2605 Brøndby (tel: 43 26 26 26).

BADMINTON

Badminton is an extremely popular sport in Denmark and most of the major towns have excellent indoor courts. These are often in heavy demand, however, and it can be difficult to find courts available. Generally, mornings are the easiest time to get in.

For further information, including details about training camps and tuition, contact:
Dansk Badminton Forbund, Idrættens Hus, Brøndby Stadion 20, DK-2605 Brøndby (tel: 43 26 26 26).

CYCLING

With its gentle undulations and extensive network of well-maintained cycle tracks, Denmark is a superb cycling country.

Dansk Cyclist Forbund (the Danish Cyclist's Association) furthers the cause of all kinds of cycling. It publishes several leaflets which are useful in the planning of a cycling holiday, such as *Cycle Tracks in Denmark*, together with route maps covering the country.

For further information contact:
Dansk Cyclist Forbund, Rømersgade 7, DK-1362, Copenhagen K (tel: 33 32 31 21).

Many local tourist offices also offer inclusive cycling holidays which can be prepaid with arrangements made in advance. The holiday will include the rent of bicycles and carriers, detailed route descriptions with maps and ferry tickets if required, plus overnight accommodation. There are reductions if you bring your own bicycle. The routes are all laid out by local experts, ensuring that, whenever possible, they follow good cycle tracks and little-used minor roads. *Contact any Danish tourist office (in Denmark or abroad) for details about these excellent holidays.*

FOOTBALL

This is the sport that excites Denmark above all others, with some 300,000 active players.

For details of major venues, where top club and international matches are played, contact:
Dansk Boldspil-Union, 1 Drettens Hus, Brøndby Stadion 20, 2605 Brøndby (tel: 43 26 22 22).

GOLF

The rolling Danish countryside is ideal for golf and there are currently 117 courses spread across the country. Foreign visitors are welcome at Danish clubs, the usual requirement being a valid membership card from their own club. Some clubs have introduced handicap restrictions, so it is a good idea to check with the club pro or secretary

Denmark takes on Nigeria

before visiting. Green fees are reasonable at around 180Dkr for 18 holes on weekdays, and around 200Dkr at weekends. Courses near large cities can be crowded on weekends and holidays.

For lists of courses, green fees and information on golfing holidays contact:
Dansk Golf Union, Idrættens Hus, Brøndby Stadion 20, DK-2605 Brøndby (tel: 43 26 26 26).

HORSE-RIDING

There are riding schools, stables and centres throughout Denmark, some of which offer special riding holidays with half or full board. Prices per hour are from around 45Dkr, and up to 125Dkr if tuition is included; day hire rates are from 20Dkr. At many centres, horse-drawn wagons can also be hired.

For further information contact:
Dansk Ride Forbund, Langebjerg 6, DK-2850 Nærum (tel: 42 80 43 44).

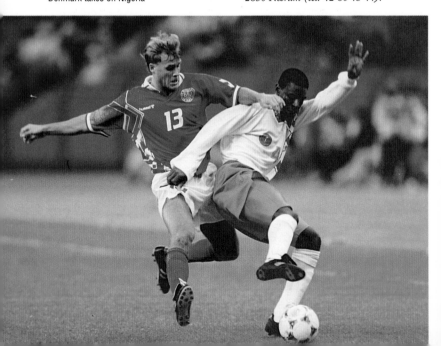

Sailing is hugely popular in Denmark with its many sheltered inlets and an extensive coastline

SAILING

With Denmark's wealth of harbours and marinas, the country offers excellent sailing facilities. Most visitors who come to Denmark specifically for a sailing holiday sail or tow their own boats.

For lists of companies offering boat hire, contact:

Dansk Sejlunion, Idrættens Hus, Brøndby Stadion 20, DK-2605 Brøndby (tel: 43 26 26 26).

Always bring certificates of competence to sail particular classes of boat.

TENNIS

Tennis is so popular all year round in Denmark that most clubs' courts, both indoor and outdoor, are in full use by members after 5pm. However, many welcome guests, particularly in off-peak hours, and visitors should contact clubs in advance. Hire costs are usually around 100Dkr for outdoor courts, and 150Dkr for indoor. Most holiday and sports centres have courts which are much more accessible and either free or relatively cheap. In most cases it is also possible to rent or borrow rackets, balls and shoes.

During the summer, grand-prix tennis tournaments are held all over the country. These allow the participation of both foreign and Danish players on application to clubs.

Further information from:

Dansk Tennis Forbund, Idrættens Hus, Brøndby Stadion 20, DK-2605 Brøndby (tel: 43 26 26 26).

WINDSURFING

This is a sport that has taken Denmark by storm in recent years. The long inlets and protected shores are excellent for beginners, while the open seas offer new challenges to experienced windsurfers.

For further information contact:

Danish Sailboard Association, Idrættens Hus, Brøndby Stadion 20, DK-2605 Brøndby (tel: 42 45 55 55).

Food and Drink

*T*he Danes do not eat out regularly, largely on account of the prohibitive prices. The top venues, as elsewhere in the world, are largely the preserve of people with expense accounts, although Danes will splash out for a special occasion, such as a birthday or a wedding anniversary. All over Denmark, however, you will find a good selection of inexpensive restaurants and cafés, many serving open sandwiches and other tasty snacks, especially at lunchtime.

PRICES

In the restaurant listings below, the following symbols have been used to indicate the average cost per person for a meal, not including alcohol.

$ – less than 75Dkr
$$ – 75–175Dkr
$$$ – 175–300Dkr
$$$$ – more than 300Dkr

Prices are inclusive of cover charge, service charge and 25 per cent purchase tax (known as MOMS). Tipping is not standard, though 'rounding up' is common practice.

The average cost of an ordinary bottle of wine in a restaurant, is in the region of 120–150Dkr.

COPENHAGEN

RESTAURANTS

Alsace $$$$
Some of the most refined French cuisine in Copenhagen. Relaxed atmosphere.
Ny Østergade 9 (tel: 33 14 57 43).

Anna N $$$$
One of Copenhagen's leading seafood specialists.
Boltens Gård, Gothersgade 10 (tel: 33 91 88 88).

Bistro $
Good-value buffet by the railway station.
DSB Restauranten, Kbh's Hovedbanegård, Banegårdspladsen 7 (tel: 33 14 12 32).

Bøf & Ost $$$
Very popular French restaurant, next door to Peder Oxe's Vinkælder (see Cafés opposite).
Gråbødretorv 13 (tel: 33 11 99 11).

Café Victor's Dining Restaurant $$
Lively and fun, serving good food at reasonable prices.
Ny Østergade 8 (tel: 33 13 36 13).

Els $$$$
Plush, traditional and expensive. Serves fine venison.
Store Strandstræde 3 (tel: 33 14 13 41).

Havfruen $$$
Excellent Danish fish restaurant on the canal.
Nyhavn 39 (tel: 33 11 11 38).

Les Etoiles $$$
Good French restaurant with selection of wines by the glass.
Dronningens Tværgade 43 (tel: 33 91 53 60).

Grøften $$$
Traditional Danish food. The best of the restaurants in the Tivoli Gardens.
Tivoli Gardens (tel: 33 12 11 25).

Kong Hans Kælder $$$
A strikingly flamboyant restaurant in a 16th-century cellar.
Vingårdstræde 6 (tel: 33 11 68 68).

Krogs Fiskerestaurant $$$
On the docks where fish has been bartered for centuries. First rate fruits of the sea.
Gammel Strand 38 (tel: 33 15 89 15).

Leonore Christine $$$$
Beautiful setting in an old house overlooking the canal. Sophisticated menu.
Nyhavn 9 (tel: 33 13 50 40).

Lumskebugten $$$
Classic Danish food in the harbour area, themed on sailing. Eat outside in fine weather.
Esplanaden 21 (tel: 33 15 60 29).

Nyhavns Færgekro $$
Excellent lunchtime buffet with copious fish. Separate à la carte restaurant.
Nyhavn 5 (tel: 33 15 15 88).

Sankt Gertruds Kloster $$$
Richly atmospheric ambience in ancient monastery cellars lit by hundreds of candles.
Hauser Plads 32 (tel: 33 14 66 30).

Spisehuset $$
Fairly simple, good-value traditional Danish food.
Rådhusstræde 13 (tel: 33 14 52 70).

When the sun shines, café life spills on to the pavements of Copenhagen

CAFÉS

Barcelona $$
Smart café serving excellent snacks.
Fælledvej 21 (tel: 31 35 76 11).

Dan Turell $$
Attracts arty types.
Sankt Regnegade 3-5 (tel: 33 14 10 47).

Peder Oxe's Vinkælder $$
Atmospheric old building. Good value buffet lunches.
Gråbrødretorv 11 (tel: 33 11 11 93).

Sabines Cafeteria $$
Fashionable stop for young 'yuppy' crowd.
Teglgårdsstræde 4 (tel: 33 14 09 44).

Somersko $$
Student café with a range of Danish and ethnic snacks.
Kronprinsensgade 6 (tel: 33 14 81 89).

Universitetscaféen $
Lively café, open till 5am.
Fiolstræde 2 (tel: 33 14 72 18).

Wilder $
Excellent place for a down-to-earth open sandwich, especially at lunchtime.
Wildersgade 56 (tel: 31 54 71 83).

Århus drinkers have a wide choice of avant-garde bars to choose from

ETHNIC

Bali $$$

Authentic Indonesian décor and excellent rice tafel.

Lille Kongensgade 4 (tel: 33 11 08 08).

Bamboo $$

Large and extremely popular central Chinese restaurant.

Rådhuspladsen 77 (tel: 33 14 40 77).

Canaletto $$$

Italian restaurant by Nyhavn canal.

Nyhavn 31 (tel: 33 14 58 44).

Govindas $$

Vegetarian restaurant serving many Indian-style dishes.

Nørre Farimagsgade 82 (tel: 33 33 74 44).

Hercegovina $$

Unusual restaurant serving Balkan dishes.

Bernstorffsgade 3 (tel: 33 15 63 63).

Kashmir $$

Excellent value Kashmiri and Indian food. Lunchtime buffet.

Nørrebrogade 35 (tel: 35 37 54 71).

Kreta $$

Good value Greek food. Lunchtime buffet.

Jagtvej 59 (tel: 31 81 77 58).

Latino $$

Small cosy restaurant serving central and south American food.

Gothersgade 113 (tel: 33 14 27 93).

Nam's Malaysian Kusine $$$

Specialises in fish served in a wide variety of spicy, oriental fashions.

Strandlinjen 49 (tel: 32 53 18 88).

Quattro Fontane $$

First-rate Italian food at good prices. Can be crowded.

Guldbergsgade 3 (tel: 31 39 39 31).

Sea Palace $$$
Up-market Chinese food on a colourful reproduction Chinese imperial ship, moored in the harbour.
Havnegade 20, Kajplads 139 (tel: 33 93 98 88).

AALBORG

RESTAURANTS
Caféen and Duffy $$
Lunchtime café and à la carte restaurant in a beautiful old house.
Jomfru Ane Gade 8 (tel: 98 16 34 44).

Duus Vinkjælder $$
Wine bar in the atmospheric vaults of Jens Bang's house which also serves meals.
9 Østerå (tel: 98 12 50 56).

Faklen $$$$
Elegant and tasteful, serving mainly French food.
Jomfru Ane Gade 21 (tel: 98 13 70 30).

Hereford Beefstow $$$
Best place in town for a hearty steak.
Ved Stranden 7 (tel: 98 12 75 22).

Kompasset $$
Pub serving meals in the maritime area. Good-value lunch snacks.
Vestre Bådehavn, Bådehavnsvej 11 (tel: 98 13 75 00).

Papegøjehaven $$
Excellent-value lunchtime buffets.
Europa Plads 2 (tel: 98 12 54 99).

Penny Lane Fish Restaurant $$$$
High-class Danish restaurant, specialising in fish, with sophisticated and elegant surroundings.
Sankelmarksgade 9 (tel: 98 12 05 80).

Prinses Juliana $$$
Danish food aboard the *Prinses Juliana*, moored at Limfjord bridge.
Limfjord (tel: 98 11 55 66).

Provence $$
French-Danish restaurant with budget lunches and a fuller range of dishes in the evenings. Good seafood.
11 Ved Stranden (tel: 98 13 51 53).

Regensen $$
Bistro-style, with a grill and a good children's menu.
Jomfru Ane Gade (tel: 98 12 59 77).

Scheelsminde $$$
Up-market restaurant serving French/Danish cuisine.
Scheelsmindevej 35 (tel: 98 18 32 33).

Sundby Hus $$$
Superb lunch venue with extensive Danish buffet.
Hjørringvej 156 (tel: 98 17 27 77).

ETHNIC
China $$
Chinese food plus a choice of international dishes.
10 Borgergade (tel: 98 13 74 80).

Fellini $$
Mainstream Italian pizza and pasta restaurant.
23 Jomfru Ane Gade (tel: 98 11 34 55).

Jules Verne $$$
Ever-changing menus from around the world.
Jomfru Ane Gade 14 (tel: 98 16 35 55).

Kinesisk Restaurant $$
Good Chinese food. Excellent crispy duck.
5 Vingårdsgade (tel: 98 13 19 11).

Kunst & Spaghetti $$
Southern Mediterranean cuisine with an arty ambience.
Vesterbro 65 (tel: 98 12 63 13).

Layalina $$$
Arabic restaurant also serving a range of international dishes.
Ved Stranden 7–9 (tel: 98 11 60 56).

La Plancha $$
Mediterranean buffet and barbecue. Eat all you want for fixed price.
Vesteraa 24 (tel: 98 12 70 73).

DANISH FOOD

A typical day's eating in Denmark is rather like a thick sandwich – a hearty breakfast and dinner, with just a sliver of lunch wedged in between. The emphasis is on fresh ingredients and simple preparation, without much recourse to the exotic. There's almost no regional variation across the country.

First, the breakfast (*morgenmad*). In hotels or inns, a typical spread will include cereal, yoghurt, cheese (usually eaten with jam!), boiled eggs, three or more different varieties of soused herring, cold meats, liver paté, a huge selection of bread (led by thick hunks of white *franskbrød* and slender slices of dark, rye *rugbrød*) and, of course, light and flaky Danish pastries. In fact, just about anything is served for breakfast except

bacon, most of which is exported.

For lunch (*frokost*, which confusingly means breakfast in other Scandinavian languages) the *smørrebrød* open sandwich reigns supreme. A thin layer of bread is topped with a choice of toppings, such as egg, cheese, salami, smoked

salmon or soused fish – either one of these, or a kaleidoscope of flavours on a single plate. *Smørrebrød* is served in a variety of sizes, as reflected in the prices, and is usually accompanied by a salad of fresh, raw vegetables.

Although sometimes

Above: in Denmark, cheese is eaten at breakfast and also plays an important part in the famous open sandwich with its myriad toppings
Left: fresh fish is readily available everywhere, and there is always something for the sweet-toothed shopper

served at lunchtime, hot dishes are generally reserved for dinner (confusingly known as *middag*). Fresh fish, simply prepared, can be outstanding; sole (*søtunge*), flounder (*hellefisk*) and halibut (*helleflynder*) from the North Sea or the Baltic can be superb steamed or lightly fried in butter and served with vegetables and excellent Danish potatoes.

By far the most common meat dish is *frikadeller*, a meatball, usually of pork mixed with flour, egg, chopped onions and herbs, served with potatoes and thick gravy. It's a great filler and good value in restaurants. Pork can be excellent; roasted loin (*helstegt svinekam*) is worth looking out for.

Meals tend to finish with fresh fruit or cheese rather than sweets. Even so, you should look out for *rødgrød med fløde* (red porridge with cream) whose notoriety owes much to the fact that foreigners find it the least pronounceable phrase in the entire Danish language.

BORNHOLM

Christianshøjkroen $$$
Serves fish, game and other Bornholm delicacies. Located out in the Almingen forest.
Segenvej 48, Aarkirkeby (tel: 56 97 40 13).

Eleonora Christina $$$$
Elegant restaurant serving gourmet Danish/French cuisine.
Strandhotellet, Sandvig, Strandpromenaden 7 (tel: 56 48 03 14).

Fyrtøjet $$
Hans Christian Andersen 'fairytale' buffets (eat all you want).
Sankt Torvegade 22, Rønne (tel: 56 95 30 12).

ESBJERG

Biografen $$
Young people's fun café serving traditional Danish food and vegetarian dishes.
Finsensgade 1 (tel: 75 45 09 22).

Brasseriet $$
Good selection of Danish and French cuisine, including a children's menu.
Torvet (tel: 75 13 01 11).

Den Grimme Aelling $$
Buffet restaurant serving a copious range of Danish dishes. Eat outside in summer.
Kirkegade 21 (tel: 75 13 54 10).

ODENSE

Asia House $$$
Broad menu of good Thai food.
Østre Stationvej 40 (tel: 66 12 19 24).

Biografen $$
Modern café with an arty environment.
Brandts Passage 39–41 (tel: 66 13 16 16).

Brandts $
Café and restaurant serving good-value lunchtime snacks.
Brandts Passage 35 (tel: 66 14 00 49).

City Cafeen $
Good value and centrally located. Sit outside in summer. Children's menu.
Vestergade 26 (tel: 66 11 92 11).

Mamma's $$
Good pizza and pasta with friendly service.
Klaregade 4 (tel: 66 14 55 40).

Prior $
Good meals all day in the heart of the city, near Hans Christian Andersen's house.
Fisketorvet 2–4 (tel: 66 12 74 94).

ÅRHUS

RESTAURANTS

Åstedet $$
Homely and traditional, serving old-fashioned Danish food.
Åboulevarden 55 (tel: 86 12 53 15).

M/F Broen $$$
Restaurant-ship moored in the harbour, offering high-quality international cuisine.
Gammel Honnørkaj 7 (tel: 86 13 14 29).

Le Canard $$$
High-quality French food in the centre of town.
Frederiksgade 74 (tel: 86 12 58 38).

DSB Restaurant $$
Bright and airy station restaurant serving traditional Danish food. Good-value lunches.
Århus Hovedbanegård (tel: 86 12 02 26).

De Fire Årstider $$$$
Up-market Danish restaurant serving excellent fish and seafood.
Åboulevarden 47 (tel: 86 19 96 96).

Eifel $$
Ultra-modern breakfast restaurant which includes a breakfast disco on certain days.
Store Torv 11 (tel: 86 20 15 66).

Hereford Beefstouw $$$
One in a nationwide chain of popular grills and steak houses.
Skolegade 5 (tel: 86 13 53 25).

Odense has a broad sweep of ethnic bars and cafés in which to while away time

Jacob's Bar BQ $$$

Large and juicy barbecued steaks served in an atmospheric old merchant's house, with courtyard.
Vestergade 3 (tel: 86 12 20 42).

Prins Ferdinand $$$$

Gourmet Danish cuisine served in sumptuous surroundings.
Den Gamle By, Viborgvej 2
(tel: 86 12 52 05).

Skovmøllen $$

Excellent Danish food served in an old water mill near Moesgard.
Skovmøllenvej 51 (tel: 86 27 12 14).

Windsor Pub $

Despite its name, very Danish and very *hygge* (cosy).
Skolebakken 17 (tel: 86 12 23 00).

ETHNIC
Chinatown $$

Authentic Chinese restaurant situated opposite the main bus station.
Fredensgade 46 (tel: 86 19 62 64).

Hong Kong $$

Hong Kong and Cantonese specialities. Good value.
Europlads 6 (tel: 86 12 32 15).

Italia $$

Pizzas cooked in a wood-fired oven. Steaks grilled at the table.
Åboulevarden 9 (tel: 86 19 80 22).

Italienske Spisehis $$

Italian restaurant at street level, with a cheaper pizzeria in the basement.
Sankt Clemens Bro 15 (tel: 86 12 08 22).

Kapadokya El Meze $$

Excellent Turkish restaurant, specialising in Anatolian food.
Klostergade 32 (tel: 86 20 94 95).

Kashmir $$

Unusual Indian and Pakistani food, at the edge of the old town.
Vesterbrogade 36 (tel: 86 13 16 37).

DRINK

Moralists who find comfort in the restrictive attitudes that prevail towards drink in other Nordic countries may be disappointed with Denmark. The anti-drink lobby simply does not exist in any comparable fashion.

Although taxes on alcohol are high, and drinks in bars and restaurants can be seriously expensive, the Danes nevertheless drink with zest. Wines, beers and spirits can be purchased in grocery stores during usual normal shopping hours, and a huge selection of bars can be found open at any time.

For Danes, beer reigns supreme. The roots of this drink are deeply implanted in Danish culture; breweries are known to have existed in the 15th century and there is evidence that fermented drinks, flavoured with hops, were being made at least 200 years earlier. Today, Carlsberg and Tuborg, the country's two most popular breweries, are both international names.

The Danes are also keen on their liqueurs, often served as chasers and knocked back with a glass of beer. Sweet brands are rarely drunk; aquavit, distilled from potatoes or grain, is preferred and is always served chilled. The drink comes in a variety of different forms, flavoured with caraway seeds, myrtle or dill and varying from colourless to pale gold. Aalborg is the main production centre. Gammel Dansk, a Danish bitter with an endless list of ingredients, has the reputation for being a good hangover remedy. Whatever the truth of this, uninitiated palates generally find its taste hard to cope with.

Wine drinking and tasting also has a strong following in Denmark. Wine merchants and restaurateurs offer a wide selection of European and New World wines. Wine-tasting societies often meet in hotels to appraise a particular vintage. Even so, the evening frequently ends up with a round of beer.

'I drink therefore I am.' Tipping back a few beers is part of Danish philosophy

Hotels and Accommodation

*H*otels in Denmark cover the full range, from sumptuous, historic five-star hotels such as Copenhagen's renowned Hotel d'Angleterre and equally luxurious modern business hotels in all the main cities, through affordable inns, farmhouses and holiday centres, to campsites or youth and family hostels for those on a budget.

The Danish Tourist Board publishes the *Denmark Accommodation Guide* listing more than 1,100 hotels, holiday centres and inns in Denmark, the Faroe Islands and Greenland. Each listing gives the hotel name, address, phone and fax numbers, capacity, facilities and prices. The guide is available free of charge from Danish Tourist Board offices, together with lists of tour operators who offer an accommodation booking service in Denmark.

COPENHAGEN

As a rough guide, prices in the capital tend to be 30–40 per cent more expensive than elsewhere. Expect to pay up to 1,900Dkr per night for a double room in a five-star hotel including breakfast, tax and service charges. At the other end of the scale, it is possible to find a simple, clean, comfortable room in a two-star, or equivalent, for 300–450Dkr.

OUTSIDE COPENHAGEN

Prices are cheaper and a full range of hotels is available in the main cities, plus various other types of accommodation, as listed below.

Camping

There are about 500 campsites in Denmark, classified by star ratings from one to three. One-star sites are rudimentary and provide just a drinking-water supply and basic washing and toilet facilities. Two-star sites are fully equipped with showers, shaving points and laundry and ironing facilities. A third star is awarded for additional facilities – often swimming pools, shops and cafés. At

The Admiral Hotel in Copenhagen

Hotels such as the Palace, in Copenhagen, come at the top of Denmark's range of accommodation

many sites it is also possible to rent caravans or cabins, where all you need bring is bed linen and towels. Campers should obtain an International Camping Carnet in their home country, or buy one at the first site they stay at.

Further information, and a copy of *Camping Denmark*, an official guide to sites with their ratings, is available from Campingrådet, Hesseløgade 16, DK-2100, Copenhagen (tel: 39 27 88 44).

Farmhouse holidays
This is an option for those who want to stay in rural Denmark, and experience real farm and family life. Guests stay in private homes, often eating with the family. When you make a booking you can request to stay on specific types of farms, or farms with facilities for children or special interests, such as fishing, walking or cycling. The cost is in the region of 250Dkr per person per day half board (full board possible). It is also possible to find self-catering cottages on farms.

For details, contact the Danish Tourist Board, or Danish Farm Holidays, Søndergade 26, DK-8700 Horsens (tel: 75 62 38 22).

Holiday centres

These self-contained resorts are found all over Denmark, though most of them are near the beach. Typically, they comprise well-kitted-out family apartments sleeping two to eight people. There is a restaurant and/or cafeteria, although kitchen facilities are available for those who want to do their own cooking. Dansk Folkeferie operates 11 holiday centres around the country. Contact them at Gammel Kongevej 33, DK-1610 Copenhagen V (tel: 33 25 33 88).

Contact the Danish Tourist Board for details of other companies and for booking forms.

A youth hostel on Jutland. The standard of Danish hostels is a cut above most others

Home exchange

By offering your own house or flat to a Danish family in the same period that you take a holiday in Denmark, the two parties simply swap homes. This can be particularly well suited to families. The coordinator tries to match families with children of the same age, so that toys, bicycles, boats or any other facilities can be shared.

Contact Dansk Boligbytte c/o Homelink International, Linfield House, Gorse Hill Road, Virginia Water, Surrey (tel: 01344 842642).

Inns

Prices are fixed at 550Dkr per double room per night, including breakfast, at Denmark's network of 86 comfortable

Seaside campers at Tranum, on Jutland. Sites come with varying facilities

and generally very friendly inns. Single or family rooms are also available. All have a bath or shower. Discounts of 10–25 per cent are offered if you pre-purchase Inn Cheques from tourist offices or from certain tour operators.

Contact Dansk Kroferie, Danish Inns Holidays, Vejlevej 16, DK-8700 Horsens (tel: 75 64 87 00).

Private homes

Staying in a private home is an option for people on a budget or interested in a more intimate experience of everyday Danish life. Breakfast is not always included but can often be arranged. Book through the local tourist office. In the UK, the service can be booked through Host and Guest Service, The Studio, Harwood House, 27 Effie Road, London SW6 1EN (tel: 0171 731 53 40).

Self-catering

Many Danish families own summer cottages, usually by a beach, which they rent out when not in use through local booking agents and tourist offices. They are well furnished and some have luxurious features such as indoor swimming pools, saunas and whirlpools. You need to bring your own towels and bed linen. An average cottage sleeping six costs upwards of 4,000Dkr per week in summer.

Youth and family hostels

Youth hostels in Denmark offer a considerably higher degree of comfort than most of their counterparts elsewhere in Europe. Many have rooms with two or four beds, plus an en suite bathroom. They can provide an excellent means for people of all ages to explore Denmark on a budget, especially families (hence the renaming of what were formerly called simply 'Youth Hostels'). A valid membership card issued by your home country's Youth Hostel Association is needed, or you can buy one from a Danish hostel. Overnight stays cost 84Dkr per person in dormitory accommodation and 150–336Dkr in private rooms. Breakfast and dinner are extra.

Contact Youth Information Centre, Use-it, Rådhusstræde 13, DK-1466 Copenhagen (tel: 33 15 65 18 for a hostels guide and map).

THOMAS COOK
Traveller's Tip

Travellers who purchase their travel tickets from a Thomas Cook network location are entitled to use the services of any other Thomas Cook network location, free of charge, to make hotel reservations.

On Business

*T*he Danes are scrupulously punctual in their business dealings. If they fore-see the likelihood of being so much as five minutes late for an appointment, they will probably telephone apologetically. Underlying this is what some people regard as an almost obsessional dependence on the telephone, with business associates sometimes speaking to each other several times a day on different topics where in other countries a single, longer call would be the more usual approach.

DRESS

In matters of dress, Danes tend to be less formal than in many parts of Europe. Blazers or sports jackets, worn with a tie, are acceptable substitutes for business suits in most instances.

BUSINESS HOURS

Normal office hours are 8 or 9am until 4 or 5pm.
Banking hours are 9.30am–4pm Monday to Friday, and to 6pm on Thursday.

CONFERENCES AND EXHIBITIONS

Copenhagen

Bella Center (tel: 32 52 88 11).
Radisson SAS Falconer Hotel & Congress Center (tel: 31 19 80 01).

Århus

Århus Congress Center
(tel: 86 13 88 44).

ECONOMIC INDICATORS 1994

Money

Inflation: 1.2%
GDP: 870 billion Dkr
GDP growth rate: 1%
Private consumption per capita: 89,000Dkr
Industrial Share Price (1985=100) April 1994: 318

As a per cent of GDP (1993)

Trade surplus: 7.7

Current Account Surplus: 3.9
General government expenditure: 60
Tax revenues: 50
General government financial deficit: 4.8

Employment

People in employment: 1,915,000
Percentage change since 1980: 9.3
Female participation 1990: 78.4 per cent of the female workforce in employment
Percentage employed in agriculture, forestry and fishing: 5.6
Percentage in industry: 27.5
Percentage in services: 66.9
Unemployment percentage: 12

SECRETARIAL SERVICES, INTERPRETERS AND TRANSLATORS

Copenhagen

Compactas (tel: 33 25 65 10).
Commercial Translation
(tel: 33 93 30 34).

Århus

Karin Lange (tel: 86 13 81 00).

MOBILE TELEPHONE RENTAL

Telecom Center, Copenhagen Airport transit area (tel: 32 52 00 22).

STOCK EXCHANGE

The KFX Index is a key index made up of the 20 most actively traded shares on the Copenhagen stock exchange.

Wheeling and dealing inside Copenhagen's modern stock exchange

Up-to-date share and bond information from the Copenhagen stock exchange can be found on Danmarks Radio teletext pages 554–63.

USEFUL ADDRESSES

Agricultural Council, 3 Axeltorv, DK-1609 Copenhagen V (tel: 33 14 56 72).

Chamber of Commerce, Børsen, DK-1217 Copenhagen K (tel: 33 95 05 00).

Confederation of Danish Industries, 18 HC Andersens Blvd, DK-1533 Copenhagen V (tel: 33 77 33 77).

Danish Bankers' Association, 7 Amaliegade, DK–1256 Copenhagen K (tel: 33 12 02 00).

Danish Employers' Federation, 113 Vester Voldgade, DK-1790 Copenhagen V (tel: 33 93 40 00).

Danish Federation of Small Industries, 15 Amaliegade, DK-1256 Copenhagen K (tel: 33 93 20 00).

Danish Federation of Trade Unions, 12 Rosenørns Allé, DK-1634 Copenhagen V (tel: 31 35 35 41).

Foreign Press Association in Denmark, Snaregade 14, DK-1205 Copenhagen K (tel: 33 13 16 15).

Industrial Fund for Central and Eastern Europe, 4 Bremerholm, DK-1069 Copenhagen K (tel: 33 14 25 75).

Ministry of Foreign Affairs, 2 Asiatisk Plads, DK-1448 Copenhagen K (tel: 33 92 00 00).

National Agency of Industry and Trade, 135 Tagensvej, DK-2200 Copenhagen N (tel: 31 85 10 66).

Practical Guide

ARRIVING

Entry formalities

Citizens of the European Union (EU) and of other Scandinavian countries do not officially require passports but must have an identity card or another accepted form of identification carrying a photograph of the holder. Citizens of all other countries require a full passport. It is recommended that the passport should have a minimum of six months validity upon entering the country.

Visas

No visas are required by citizens of Australia, Canada, New Zealand and the USA for stays of up to 90 days. Citizens of the Republic of South Africa require a visa.

By air

Copenhagen's Kastrup International is one of Europe's most modern and efficient airports, with connections to more than 70 countries worldwide on some 40 different airlines. It is the principal hub for Scandinavian Airline Systems (SAS: in the UK tel: 0171 734 4020), the airline that operates as joint national carrier for Denmark, Norway and Sweden.

Maersk Air (in the UK tel: 0171 333 0066) flies between Denmark and a variety of other European destinations including London Gatwick.

Danair offers services within Denmark. AirUK (in the UK tel: 01345 666777) flies daily from London Stansted. There are also flights to Copenhagen from Birmingham, Manchester and Glasgow.

Kastrup is about 10km southeast of Copenhagen; SAS buses operate a frequent and inexpensive service into the city centre.

There are direct flights on SAS to Tirstrup Airport at Århus from London Heathrow and other European airports; there is a regular bus service from the airport into town. Maersk Air flies daily from London Gatwick to Billund, in the

Maersk Air is one of the airlines offering flights between Denmark and other countries in Europe

middle of Jutland, a few minutes' walk away from Legoland. There are also flights to Esbjerg from Aberdeen, Dundee and Humberside.

Full information on airlines and destinations serving Denmark is available from Danish National Tourist Offices.

By sea

Denmark is connected to Norway, Sweden, Germany and Britain by an intricate network of car and passenger ferries serving many ports. Scandinavian Seaways (in the UK tel: 01225 240240) sail every other day to Esbjerg from Harwich during summer and three times in winter. Crossings take about 20 hours. Full details of all sea connections from Danish National Tourist Offices.

By rail

There are direct train services to Denmark from Germany and using boat trains, from Norway, Sweden and the UK. Inter-Rail tickets are valid in Denmark.

The *Thomas Cook European Timetable* is published monthly and gives up-to-date details of most rail services and many shipping services throughout Europe; this will help plan a rail journey to, from and around Denmark. It is available in the UK from some railway stations, any branch of Thomas Cook or by phoning 01733 268943. In the USA, contact the Forsyth Travel Library Inc, 9154 West 57th St, PO Box 2957, Shawnee Mission, Kansas 66201; tel: (800) 367 7982 (toll-free).

By road

There is a motorway border crossing with Germany near Frøslev and seven other road frontiers in south Jutland. For Zealand, drivers from Germany can take a ferry from Puttgarden via Lolland Island, or Warnemünde via Falster Island.

CAMPING

See Hotels and Accommodation page 172.

CHILDREN

Facilities for children are among the best in the world (see pages 156). Many museums and other tourists attractions offer reduced or free admission to children. Many attractions provide play areas complete with toys.

CLIMATE

Denmark has a relatively mild maritime climate, generally free of extremes. Summers are usually warm and sunny, although rain is a possibility at any time of year. Winters can be cold, with the probability of snow between late December and February, though it is seldom severe. May and June can be delightful, although the likelihood of rain is greater at this time than later in the summer. July and August are the peak months for tourism.

Tourists enjoying the sea at Grenen

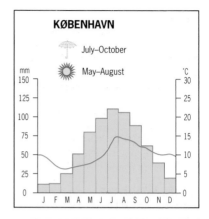

KØBENHAVN

July–October

May–August

WEATHER CONVERSION CHART
25.4mm = 1 inch
°F = 1.8 x °C = 32

CONVERSION TABLES

See opposite.

CRIME

Denmark is a very safe country and crime is rarely a problem for tourists. Nevertheless, nobody should be lulled into a false sense of security; cars should always be left locked, and luggage and other valuables removed from sight. As in most European cities, drugs-related crime is on the increase in Copenhagen and care should be taken at night, particularly round the railway station and in the vicinity of Christiania. If you are robbed, report the incident to the police immediately and ask for a copy of the statement; this will be needed for any insurance claim.

CUSTOMS REGULATIONS

Visitors to Denmark arriving from another European Union (EU) member country need not complete customs formalities. Non-EU visitors should check notices on points of entry for quantities of tobacco, wine, spirits, beer, foodstuffs and other goods for which there are entry restrictions.

DISABLED TRAVELLERS

'Denmark is a dream for disabled travellers' (authentic quote from a wheelchair user). Facilities are second to none, with most good hotels, airports, railway stations and trains, ferries terminals and ferries, museums and public toilets having access for the disabled. The Danish Tourist Board publishes *Access in Denmark – A Travel Guide for the Disabled* – a free booklet listing facilities for the disabled throughout the country, including the distance between tourist attractions and their car parks. Also contact Danish Handicap Association, Hans Knudsens Plads 1A, DK-2100 Copenhagen Ø ª tel: 39 29 35 55).

Conversion Table

FROM	TO	MULTIPLY BY
Inches	Centimetres	2.54
Feet	Metres	0.3048
Yards	Metres	0.9144
Miles	Kilometres	1.6090
Acres	Hectares	0.4047
Gallons	Litres	4.5460
Ounces	Grams	28.35
Pounds	Grams	453.6
Pounds	Kilograms	0.4536
Tons	Tonnes	1.0160

To convert back, for example from centimetres to inches, divide by the number in the the third column.

Men's Suits

UK	36	38	40	42	44	46	48
Rest of Europe	46	48	50	52	54	56	58
US	36	38	40	42	44	46	48

Dress Sizes

UK	8	10	12	14	16	18
France	36	38	40	42	44	46
Italy	38	40	42	44	46	48
Rest of Europe	34	36	38	40	42	44
US	6	8	10	12	14	16

Men's Shirts

UK	14	14.5	15	15.5	16	16.5	17
Rest of Europe	36	37	38 39/40	41		42	43
US	14	14.5	15	15.5	16	16.5	17

Men's Shoes

UK	7	7.5 8.5		9.5	10.5	11
Rest of Europe	41	42	43	44	45	46
US	8	8.5 9.5		10.5	11.5	12

Women's Shoes

UK	4.5	5	5.5	6	6.5	7
Rest of Europe	38	38	39	39	40	41
US	6	6.5	7	7.5	8	8.5

DRIVING

Denmark has an excellent network of uncluttered roads which amply supports the relatively sparse traffic. One of the best means of touring Denmark with time on your hands is to follow the Marguerit-rute (Marguerite Route) – over 3,400km of minor roads and winding lanes reaching every forgotten corner of the country. Distinctive brown, white and yellow signs point the way from just about everywhere in Denmark.

Accidents and breakdowns

All accidents must be reported to the Dansk Forening for International Motorkøretøjsforsikring, Amaliegade 10, DK-1256 Copenhagen (tel: 33 13 75 55). If another vehicle is involved, insurance details should be swapped with the other driver. Notify your insurer as soon as possible. In case of serious accident, phone 112 (toll free) for the emergency services as soon as possible.

If you break down, call one of the two national organisations, Falck or Dansk Autohjalp, which operate a 24-hour service from over 100 centres, for which you will be charged. If necessary, they will tow you to a garage. On motorways, both organisations can be called from the emergency telephones. If you need a repair and can get your own car to a garage, find one listed under Automobil reparation in the *Yellow Pages* phone book.

Alcohol

Drink–driving offences are punished by strict penalties. Driving after consuming any quantity of alcohol is illegal.

Documents

If you bring your own car into Denmark from abroad, you will need a full (not provisional) UK or EU driving licence and the car's registration documents. A green card is also highly recommended, though not required by law. A nationality badge or sticker must be displayed on the rear of the vehicle.

Fuel

The majority of fuel stations in Denmark are self-service; some are unattended, with automatic pumps accepting 100 and 50Dkr notes as payment. Leaded petrol is available (*super benzin* 98 octane) and three unleaded grades (*blyfri* – available in 98, 95 and 92 octanes). Diesel is also sold at all fuel stations.

Laws

Drive on the right and overtake on the left. Unless otherwise indicated, give way to traffic on the right. At junctions and roundabouts give way to pedestrians crossing the road you are entering. Front seat-belts must be worn, as well as back seat-belts if fitted. Also pay atention to cyclists, often using the far-right lane in cities, who have the right of way.

Unless otherwise stated, speed limits are 50kph (31mph) in built-up areas, 80kph (50mph) outside built-up areas and 100kph (62mph) on motorways. For anyone towing a caravan or other trailer, the maximum speed limit is 70kph (44mph). Built-up areas are signalled by town name signs which also have a silhouette of buildings. A similar sign with a diagonal red line through it signals the end of the built-up area limit.

Lights

As in other Scandinavian countries, it is compulsory to use dipped headlights whenever the car is being driven. This applies no matter how bright the sunlight. Drivers of right-hand-drive vehicles must use beam deflectors; (these are widely available in motoring shops and at Channel ports).

Motorcycling

Helmets must be worn at all times by riders and pillion passengers. As with other vehicles, dipped headlights should be used at all times.

Motoring organisations

The main Danish motoring organisation is the Forenede Danske Motorejere, Firskovvej 32, PO Box 500, DK-2800 Lyngby (tel: 45 93 08 00). The FDM offers legal and technical assistance to members of organisations affiliated to the AIT (Alliance Internationale de Tourisme) including Britain's Automobile Association (the AA).

Parking

Danish cars are fitted with parking dials (called P-Skive), resembling a clock, displayed on the front windscreen or dashboard. If you are bringing your own car into the country, stop and get one, free of charge, at any fuel station. In many towns parking is free for a finite period as indicated by signs such as *2 timer* (2 hours); set the dial to the nearest quarter of an hour to your arrival time, and be sure to move on before the indicated span of time has expired.

Other towns have pay-and-display car parks (*Parkeringsbillet påkrævet*). In these, stickers are purchased from a machine and displayed on the windscreen interior.

Rental

Large international companies and smaller local ones are widely advertised and easy to find, although charges are relatively high. It can be cheaper to book a car in advance from your home country. By law, you must be over 20 years old to hire a car, but some companies insist on drivers being at least 23, and sometimes 25.

Danish police enforce strict penalties for drink-driving

ELECTRICITY

The electric current is 220 volts AC (50Hz) and sockets are for continental two-point plugs. An adaptor will be needed for UK appliances fitted with a three-point plug, and a voltage transformer for appliances from the USA and Canada.

EMBASSIES AND CONSULATES

Australia 21 Kristianiagade, DK–2100 Copenhagen (tel: 35 26 22 44).
Canada 1 Kristen Bernikows Gade, DK-1105 Copenhagen (tel: 33 12 22 99).
Republic of Ireland Østbanegade 21, DK-2100 Copenhagen (tel: 31 42 32 33).
United Kingdom 36–40 Kastelsvej, DK-2100 Copenhagen Ø (tel: 35 26 46 00).
USA 24 Dag Hammerskjolds Allé, DK-2100 Copenhagen Ø (tel: 31 42 31 44).

EMERGENCY TELEPHONE NUMBERS

Accidents, police, fire or ambulance: 112 (toll free from public call boxes.)

The Thomas Cook Worldwide Customer Promise offers free emergency assistance at any Thomas Cook Network location to travellers who have purchased their travel tickets at a Thomas Cook Network location. In addition, any MasterCard holder may use any Thomas Cook Network location to report loss or theft of their card and obtain an emergency card replacement, as a free service under the Thomas Cook MasterCard International Alliance. Currently there are no Network locations in Denmark, but this will change. Travellers from the UK can check the latest position by phoning 0171 408 4107.

Thomas Cook MasterCard Refund Centre (24-hour service – report loss or theft within 24 hours, tel: 80 01 01 10).

LANGUAGE

Danish is a Germanic language, close to Swedish and Norwegian, and many words are similar to German. But it is a difficult language to pronounce because some letters (d, g) are silent in the middle or at the end of words, h before a v becomes silent, and some specifically Scandinavian vowels (æ,ø, å), are awkward to say correctly. But the Danes are aware of this problem and most speak very good English. The following words should help you to get around and read menus (which are often also in English and German).

yes	ja
no	nej
please	vær så
thank you	venlig
hello	hej
goodbye	farvel
good morning	godmorgen
good afternoon	goddag
good evening	godaften
good night	godnat
entrance	indgang
no entry	ingen adgang (for pedestrians)
exit	udgang
no exit	ingen udgang
emergency exit	nødudgang
push/pull	skub/træk or tryk/træk
ladies	damer
gentlemen	herrer
toilets	toiletter
open	åben
close	lukket
no smoking	rygning forbudt
arrival	ankomst

departure	afgang		**pork**	flæsk, svine
timetable	køreplan		**chicken**	kylling
townplan	bykort		**boiled chicken**	høne/hønse
step down/up	trin ned /op		**white bread**	franskbrød
no standing	rejs Dem ikke op		**rye bread**	rugbrød
			French bread	flûte
Monday	mandag		**Danish pastry**	Wienerbrød
Tuesday	tirsdag		**butter**	smør
Wednesday	onsdag		**shellfish**	skaldyr
Thursday	torsdag		**herring**	sild
Friday	fredag		**trout**	ørred
Saturday	lørdag		**cod**	torsk
Sunday	søndag		**shrimps**	rejer
			vegetables	grøntsager
opening times	åbningstider		**onion**	løg
o'clock	klokken		**peas**	ærter
exhibition	udstilling		**potatoes**	kartofler
petrol	benzin		**red cabbage**	rødkål
car	bil		**carrot**	gulerod
do not touch	må ikke berøres		**cheese**	ost
railway	station banegård		**fruit salad**	frugtsalat
railway line	jernbane			
street	gade		**coffee/tea**	kaffe/the
ferry	færge		**house wine**	husets vin
no entry	(cars) ingen indkørsel		**red/white**	rød/hvid
Great Britain	Storbritannien		**apple juice**	æblemost
USA	De Forenede Stater		**orange juice**	appelsinjuice
			full cream milk	sødmælk
			less fatty milk	letmælk
	Food		**skimmed milk**	skummetmælk
breakfast	morgenmad			
lunch	frokost			
dinner	middagsmad		**Numbers**	
starters	forretter		**1**	en
soups	supper		**2**	to
main courses	hovedretter		**3**	tre
fish dishes	fiskeretter		**4**	fire
cold dishes	fra det kolde køkken		**5**	fem
hot dishes	fra det varme køkken		**6**	seks
baked	bagt		**7**	syv
roast	helstegt, steg		**8**	otte
steamed	dampet		**9**	ni
smoked	røget		**10**	ti

A cosmopolitan selection of publications is to be found on city news-stands

HEALTH

There are no mandatory vaccination requirements. It is recommended that travellers keep tetanus and polio immunisation up to date. As with every other part of the world, AIDS is present. Food and water are considered safe.

All EU countries have reciprocal arrangements for reclaiming the cost of medical services. UK residents should obtain forms CM1 and E111 from any post office in the UK. These provide detailed information on how to claim and what is covered. Claiming is often a long drawn-out process and you are only covered for medical care, not for emergency repatriation, holiday cancellation and so on. You are therefore strongly advised to take out a travel insurance policy to cover all eventualities. Such insurance can be purchased through the AA, branches of Thomas Cook and most travel agents.

HITCH-HIKING

Hitching is not widely practiced in Denmark and is seldom worth the effort. It is illegal on motorways.

INSURANCE

Travel insurance should be taken out before leaving to cover property loss and theft, as well as medical costs and accident cover. For drivers, third-party cover is the legal minimum but fully comprehensive cover is advisable.

LANGUAGE

See pages 184–5.

MAPS

Maps are available from tourist offices all over Denmark, generally free of charge. Some can also be obtained from Danish Tourist Board Offices in your home country.

MEDIA

Various European newspapers are available in Copenhagen and other cities from the afternoon of the day of publication.

English-language satellite television stations are received in most good hotels.

Radio Denmark broadcasts news in English from Monday to Friday at 8.30am on Programme 1 (94.5 MHz).

MONEY MATTERS

The currency is the Danish kroner (Dkr), divided into 100 øre. Banknotes are issued in 1,000, 500, 100 and 50 kroner denominations, and coins in 20, 10, 5 and 1 kroner, plus 50 and 25 øre.

Currency exchange

Outside bank opening hours (see below), money can be exchanged in most good hotels. Money can also be changed out of hours at Copenhagen's railway station, at the Magasin and Salling department stores in Århus and at the Aalborg tourist office.

Credit cards and cheques

International credit and charge cards are widely accepted throughout Denmark. Thomas Cook MasterCard travellers' cheques free you from the hazards of carrying large sums of cash, and in the event of loss or theft can be quickly refunded. US dollar and Deutschemark travellers' cheques are recommended, though cheques in other major currencies are accepted. Hotels and restaurants will generally accept travellers' cheques in lieu of cash; good quality shops may do the same.

Cash machines

Automatic cash dispensers (called *kontanten*), to be found in Copenhagen and other major cities, can be used to draw Danish currency with Eurocheque and Visa credit and charge cards.

Taxes

Many good-quality shops operate a tax refund system (see page 143).

NATIONAL HOLIDAYS

1 January New Year's Day
Maundy Thursday
Good Friday
Easter Sunday
Easter Monday
Fourth Friday after Good Friday
Great Prayer Day
Fortieth day after Easter Ascension Day
Fiftieth day after Easter Whit Monday
5 June Constitution Day
24 December Christmas Eve
25 December Christmas
26 December St Stephen
31 December New Year's Eve

OPENING HOURS
Shops

Shopping hours vary between towns. In Copenhagen, typical opening times are 10am–5.30pm Monday to Friday and 10am–1pm on Saturday. On the Strøget in July and August, however, many shops are open until late, seven days a week.

In most other cities and towns, shops open from 9 or 10am to 5.30pm Monday to Thursday, staying open later on Fridays, and from 9am–1pm on Saturdays. On the first and last Saturday of each month many shops open 4–5pm.

Banks

Banking hours are 9.30am–4pm Monday to Friday. Unibank stays open till 5pm, and all banks are open till 6pm on Thursday.

PHARMACIES

Most towns have a centrally located *apotek* (pharmacy) open during normal shopping hours, although larger cities will have one open 24 hours. These are generally listed in tourist leaflets.

It is important that travellers bring a supply of prescribed medicines to cover their entire stay in Denmark, as pharmacists may only dispense medicines prescribed by Scandinavian doctors.

The cathedral at Ribe. Many admire the architecture, but fewer worship God

PLACES OF WORSHIP

Although religious observance is minimal in Denmark, Sunday services are held in churches throughout the country.

In Copenhagen, church services are conducted in English for the following Christian denominations: International Baptist, First Church of Christ Scientist, Church of England, Methodist, International Pentecostal and Roman Catholic. Times are published in *Copenhagen This Week*, available from the tourist office free of charge.

SENIOR CITIZENS

Recipients of state pensions in their home countries are entitled to reductions on Danish railways on presentation of their passport and a senior citizen travel card. All UK travellers over 60 who hold a Senior Railcard are eligible for a 30 per cent discount on Danish railways.

TELEPHONES

The Danes are enthusiastic and frequent users of the telephone, and the country has an efficient system both for internal and international calls. Mark-ups in hotels are often exorbitant, so it is much cheaper to use a public payphone; many hotels have these in their lobbies. Operating Danish payphones is straightforward; most have instructions in English.

To dial abroad from Denmark, first dial 009, then the country code (61 for Australia, 1 for Canada or the USA, 64 for New Zealand, 353 for the Republic of Ireland, 27 for the Republic of South Africa and 44 for the United Kingdom), then the area code (omitting the initial zero) followed by the number.

Denmark's country code is 45.

TIME

From the last Saturday in September to the last Sunday in March, Denmark is on GMT plus 1 hour (ie 1 hour ahead of Britain and Ireland, 5 hours ahead of US Eastern Standard Time and 14 hours behind Sydney). In summer the clocks go forward by an hour to GMT plus 2 hours.

TIPPING

Tipping is not the norm in Denmark. Service is already included in restaurant bills and taxi fares.

TOILETS

Public toilets (*toiletter*) are among the cleanest in Europe and generally free of charge. They are segregated into men and women (*Damer/Herrer*) as indicated by the standard international pictographs.

TOURIST OFFICES

Denmark has an excellent network of tourist information offices (*Turistinformationen*). Most towns have a centrally located and well signposted office, always with English-speaking staff. As well as providing information they will book local accommodation for no charge. The address and telephone numbers of tourist offices are given in the relevant gazetteer section of this guide.

Equally efficient and helpful are the Danish Tourist Board Offices abroad:

Canada Danish Tourist Board, PO Box 115, Station N, Toronto ONT M8V 3S4 (tel: 416 823 9620).
UK (including Ireland) Danish Tourist Board, 55 Sloane Street, London SW1X 9SY(tel: 0171 259 5959).
USA Danish Tourist Board, 655 Third Avenue, New York, NY 10017 (tel: 212 949 2333).

Even dogs are provided with clean free toilets, though the sexes are not segregated

ACKNOWLEDGEMENTS
The Automobile Association wishes to thank the following photographers, libraries and associations for their assistance in the preparation of this book.

H C ANDERSENS HUS, ODENSE 80, 81a, 81b, 81c
CLAUSHOLM SLOT 93a
DANISH TOURIST BOARD 2 (T Nebbia), 17 (Lennard), 52a (J Sommer), 61b, 72 (Lennard), 82a (Preben Eider), 93b (Lennard), 131 (Wedigo Ferchland), 147 (Lennard)
MARY EVANS PICTURE LIBRARY 8, 10/11, 10
MAERSK AIR 179
MUSEUM EROTICA 35b
MUSIKHISTORISK MUSEET 34
NATURE PHOTOGRAPHERS LTD 136 (R O Bush), 138b (C Carver)
K NAYLOR 126, 173
PICTURES COLOUR LIBRARY Cover inset
SPECTRUM COLOUR LIBRARY 35a, 121, 149
STOREBÆLT 68/9, 69 (Jan Kofod Winther), 68 (Soren Madsen)
M SYMINGTON 6, 129, 134, 135a, 135b
ZEFA PICTURES LTD Cover, spine, 55, 94a, 94b, 132, 133

All remaining pictures are held in the Association's own library (AA PHOTO LIBRARY) and were taken by Jesper Westley Jorgensen with the exception of pages 13, 21a, 21b, 23, 41, 50, 54, 78, 84, 88, 91, 101, 107, 141, 147a, 172 and 174, which were taken by Derek Forss.

The author wishes to thank Ms Britt Sander of the Danish Tourist Board in London for her help during the preparation of the book and Maersk Air and Air UK for helping with travel arrangements to Denmark.

CONTRIBUTORS
Series adviser: Melissa Shales   **Designer:** Design 23   **Copy editor:** Christopher Catling
Verifier: Jenny Fry   **Indexer:** Marie Lorimer